# Rebuking the Spirit of Pride

Charles Smith

Rebuking the Spirit of Pride
Copyright ©2022 by Charles Smith

Critical Mass Books
Haymarket, Virginia
www.criticalmasspublishing.com

1st Edition

ISBN: 978-1-947153-42-4

Cover Design Eowyn Riggins
Interior Layout Rachel Newhouse

# CONTENTS

**CHAPTER ONE** ..................................................................1
*"Original Sin; On-Going Problem"*

**CHAPTER TWO** ..................................................................5
*"Of Fire and the Altar"*

**CHAPTER THREE** ............................................................11
*"Be Like Jesus"*

**CHAPTER FOUR** ..............................................................19
*"It's About Jesus"*

**CHAPTER FIVE** ................................................................25
*"There is Only One Road"*

**CHAPTER SIX** ..................................................................33
*"Check My Heart, Lord"*

**CHAPTER SEVEN** ............................................................39
*"Holier than Thou"*

**CHAPTER EIGHT** ............................................................47
*"He is God, and We Are Not"*

**CHAPTER NINE** ..............................................................57
*"We Don't Have to Know Everything"*

**CHAPTER TEN** ................................................................65
*"We Can Rest in His Assurance"*

**CHAPTER ELEVEN** ........................................................73
*"Which One Will You Choose?"*

CHAPTER TWELVE .......................................................... 79
*"No More Denial"*

CHAPTER THIRTEEN ..................................................... 85
*"Help Us, Lord!"*

CHAPTER FOURTEEN ..................................................... 91
*"A False Sense of Maturity"*

CHAPTER FIFTEEN .......................................................... 97
*"Self-Will and Stubbornness"*

CHAPTER SIXTEEN ........................................................ 103
*"We Are Called to Walk By Faith"*

CHAPTER SEVENTEEN ................................................. 109
*"Choose to Rebuke Pride and Follow God"*

CHAPTER EIGHTEEN ..................................................... 115
*"As Long As It Is Pleasing to the Lord"*

CHAPTER NINETEEN .................................................... 121
*"We Don't Have to Promote Ourselves"*

CHAPTER TWENTY ........................................................ 127
*"We Don't Need to Join Every Argument"*

## CHAPTER ONE
### *"Original Sin; On-Going Problem"*

Years ago, shortly after I became a preacher, I had a dream about catching a big fish. It was a giant brim, a freshwater fish also known as a bluegill. I love brim, but for some reason, in my dream, I took a sword and thrust it into the fish, turning it into a snake.

I'm not a big fan of snakes, but I know the meaning of that dream.

The sword represented the Word of God, and it will always reveal what's really there.

> *"For the word of God is quick, and powerful, and sharper than any two-edged sword, piercing even to the dividing asunder of soul and spirit, and of the joints and marrow, and is a discerner of the thoughts and intents of the heart."*
>
> —HEBREWS 4:12

Something may look real and that it is on the way to becoming something for the Lord, but the Sword of the Lord will always get to the truth. I am so thankful for that revelation. And I am so grateful that we have the privilege to pray. No one is greater than their prayer life. If you can't pray, you can't preach. If you can't pray, you can't witness.

And the key to effective prayer is *humility*.

*"God resisteth the proud, but giveth grace unto the humble. Submit yourselves therefore to God. Resist the devil, and he will flee from you. Draw nigh to God, and He will draw night to you. Cleanse your hands, ye sinners; and purify your hearts, ye double minded."*

—JAMES 4:6-8

Humility and pride are polar opposites. The presence of one chases the other away. Pride can make us think we are fine—everything is okay. Pride is a terrible thing and a horrible spirit. It is a powerful tool in the hand of the enemy. And like a principality or power, it must be exposed and cast out.

Pride is no respecter of persons. It's a one-size-fits all garment. No one has immunity to it. We are all subject to its toxic poison. If you don't get pride out of the way, you will never really care about others. Pride will make you feel entitled. It will rear its ugly head and embarrass you at the most inopportune times.

What was the original sin? You may think it was when Adam and Eve ate the forbidden fruit back in the Garden of Eden. But it wasn't. In fact, the first sin was committed long before that—by an angel named Lucifer.

> *"How art thou fallen from heaven, O Lucifer, son of the morning! how art thou cut down to the ground, which didst weaken the nations! For thou hast said in thine heart, I will ascend into heaven, I will exalt my throne above the stars of God: I will sit also upon the mount of the congregation, in the sides of the north: I will ascend above the heights of the clouds; I will be like the Most High. Yet thou shalt be brought down to hell, to the sides of the pit.*
>
> —ISAIAH 14:12-14

The original sin was *pride*.

It has been around since before the foundation of the world and remains an ever-present problem infecting all aspects of modern life. We feel good about ourselves when we cry out against the sins of society. But are we willing to apply the same standard the grandfather of all wickedness—pride?

We need to rebuke the spirit of pride in our own lives!

## CHAPTER TWO
*"Of Fire and the Altar"*

Pride shows up in many ways in our hearts and in our lives. Even the prideful thought that others are acting proud. We often want to point out and rebuke the sin of pride in those around us but are not willing to look at own hearts. We need a spiritual MRI so God can reveal our own prideful spirit.

Pride cuts deep. I don't want to walk around in pride. I want revival. And the only way to really experience revival is by humbling ourselves. We need to put ourselves in a place where we can pray and seek God.

William J. Seymour led the Azusa Street Revival back in 1906, and that was Ground Zero for the rise of the Pentecostal and Charismatic Movements. He was a humble man minus any hint of pride. God used him in a powerful way. One the platform, he put his head between two crates and fervently prayed. This was not for show. He wasn't trying to exalt himself. He only wanted what God wanted. We need to be like him and others like Paul and John the Baptist, who said, *"He must increase, but I must decrease."*[1] Only when we choose to decrease can God increase His presence in us. Less of me. More of Him.

If we are not careful, we will live a life where our ears are fine tuned to hear only the good things about ourselves and the affirmations of others. Too often we take great care to only seek out people who say good things about us. It is dangerous to long for people to puff us up.

At some point as followers of the Lord, there comes a time where we will offend others. When we follow God's way and His rules, according to His Word, people will always be offended. Some people would rather not take a stand and offend anyone because they have too much pride. They care too much about what others may think or say. They don't want anyone to be upset with them.

When it comes to the work of the Lord, I really don't mind offending. Offenses will come when we speak the truth in love. We must be willing to do anything for the Lord. And to do that, we must get rid of self. Paul says that we must die to ourselves daily. We must doubt our own will and submit ourselves to God. We must become sacrifices on the altar before the Lord.

A long time ago, the Lord told me that the fire needs to be back on the altar. I'm not sure if we have the right fire on the altar of our hearts. The fire on our heart's altar may not be the fire that He wants. Sometimes we need to get a word and work that word no matter what anyone else says.

Not everyone is looking for that fire. Not everyone wants to follow Jesus the way you want to follow Him. Some people want a temporary Jesus, one they can check in with a couple days a week. Not me.

I want Jesus every day.

Some people don't want the anointing of God. They only want to feel a touch when they show up. But I want His anointing every day. I want Him to consume me. I want to be saturated with the blessings of the Lord. I want all the gifting, calling, and anointing He desires for me.

Some people don't want that fire. Some people just want to hang around near the fire. They just want to be close to the smoke. They want a tiny bit of the smoldering ash of the mighty fire of God. Some people just want to simmer. But God is looking for people who are ready to burn with passion in His anointing. He's looking for people who are all in and ready to sell out. He wants people who are ready to give up everything to receive what He has for them.

Not everyone who claims to be a Christian is going to seek Him to that level. Not everyone is going to humble themselves to wait on the Lord. Too many are satisfied with the way they are. But I'm not satisfied to stay the same old me. I want that fire. I want more. I want a double portion. I want more prayer time. I want to give up more of the carnal so that I can receive more of the spiritual, like the saints of old.

Back then, they wouldn't even turn on a television because they were hearing from God. But we have drifted away from that level of devotion in our society. Watching television is not a sin. But to get something from God, we have to give up some things. We must rebuke the spirit of pride that keeps us from leaning into and seeking after God's full plan for our lives.

## What Does it Mean to Rebuke?

A rebuke is a rejection, as well as a correction, of what someone says or does. And that's what we have to do with the enemy. When we hear his lies, we need to refuse to receive them. We turn it all around and acknowledge that we will not receive what he says. That's what we must do with the spirit of pride.

When pride tries to talk to us, it always wants to deceive. Have you ever heard the voice of pride talking to you? It might say, "You don't have to take that," or "You're better than that."

I've had pride talk to me when I didn't hear God talking to me. You see, God wants to talk to us. But the spirit of pride that we have from birth and the nature of Adam grew in us. It makes us feel entitled. "I don't have to take that." "I don't have to deal with them."

It all starts small, but as we go further into our sin and pride, we start amplifying our salvation and our walk with God and we put ourselves in a place God didn't put us. We say we are "this" or "that." And we love the scriptures that say "I'm the head and not the tail. I'm above and not beneath." But sometimes we need to be beneath so that He can pull us up—and out.

We love Ephesians 3:20, where it talks about God doing exceedingly and abundantly above all that we ask or think. And we stop there. But if we keep going, we see that it is according to His power that dwells in us. He doesn't do anything except that which is according to what is dwelling in us. So often we want God to do amazing things in our lives, but we haven't done anything to warrant that power to dwell in us. We give 25% but want Him to return to us 75%.

We sometimes get puffed up because we pay our tithe. We tell the Lord that since we did our part, He needs to do this, that, or the other thing. We have a list of our expectations from God. And when they don't work out according to our wants and desires because we've done something for Him, we start to feel resentment. We say, "God, I'm in Your word and I'm feeding the people, why aren't you doing this for me?" Well, while you are doing that work are you doing it for the right reasons? Or do you have the spirit of pride? Are you doing for a reward instead of out of your love for God?

## CHAPTER THREE
### *"Be Like Jesus"*

*"Submit yourselves therefore to God. Resist the devil, and he will flee from you. Draw nigh to God, and he will draw nigh to you. Cleanse your hands, ye sinners; and purify your hearts, ye double minded."*

—JAMES 4:7-8 (KJV)

Submitting means to humble your yourself, to come under. It means to get in a subordinate position. Without that we have no power to resist the devil. Without submission, we are, in fact, telling God how to run our lives, who to send our way, which path we are supposed to be choosing, and what we want Him to give us. We want control. But when temptation arises, we want His help so we can have authority to resist the devil so that he will run away.

It doesn't work that way.

We want to put the devil on the run, but we also want to maintain control over our lives and how things should go. We want to have authority over a spirit that is trying to take authority over us, without submitting to the One who has ultimately authority. That's not going to work. The steps are all out of order.

We must start with submission. Then, resist the devil and he will flee from you. By the way, we are not told that the devil will be gone forever. But he will go away. If he comes back, we simply repeat the process and do what got rid of him the first time. Submit yourself to God, resist the devil and he will flee—that's the formula for victory.

I submit myself to God in prayer. I submit myself to God in faithfulness. I submit myself to God by giving. I submit myself to God by obeying His word. I submit myself to God by loving the people of God. Submit myself to God by loving those who hate me. I must keep submitting myself to God if I want to get rid of this enemy. When you draw near to God, He draws near to you.

God sees the heart. We don't have to be perfect. We just have to be honest and seek God above all else. He sees us trying and knows the heart. He sees our sincerity. He hears our humble prayers. He sees our unselfish motives when we aren't just praying for material things and what we can get from Him. He sees our desire for a closer walk with Him.

And He keeps His word.

Jesus told us that when we hunger and thirst after righteousness we shall be filled. We need to be humbled. And whatever you do, don't ask Him to humble you. That's like asking for patience. No. We humble ourselves. We ask Him to make us humble like Jesus. That doesn't mean that we must let someone nail us to a cross. No. That was finished more than 2000 years ago. But there are other ways to become more Christlike. Jesus rebuked pride by the way that He lived.

Think about the stories of Jesus that you know.

When the religious leaders brought a woman caught in the very act of sin, they were proud and lifted up and had rocks in their hands. They knew they were better than her, and they were going to do what Moses' law said and stone her right in front of everybody.

We can learn what not to do from them.


Be careful about thinking you have reached a level of being saved that makes you above sin. You think you got it going on. You think you are doing God a favor by stopping other sinners. Be careful when you find something out about a person and how you handle that person in conversation.

Maybe they don't know how to do something you excel at. Don't talk about them as if they are stupid. Don't feel superior to them because you have reached a level that you have reached. Don't be puffed up with pride because someone sins differently than you. Because we are all guilty of something.

You know exactly what I am talking about.

You may not want to admit it, but you can feel that spirit of recognition and authority rising up. It feels good. That is, until you come across someone who you view as better than you—someone who has accomplished more or who hasn't made the mistakes that you have. Then you flip to the other side of the coin and feel inferior, which is just a reverse pride. You think people don't like you. You feel sorry for yourself and have a pity party.

Watch how you treat people. If a person hasn't had the advantages that you have, treat them as you would hope someone would treat you. Don't embarrass them and make it all about how good you are, with your head swelled up and only looking for recognition and glory. That's the spirit of pride. God doesn't like it. Do it gently and out of public view. Do it with humility. Be like Jesus.

Christ's life rebuked pride. The life and death of our Lord Jesus Christ were an enduring rebuke to every form of pride.

There is pride of *birth*: "Is not this the carpenter's son?"[2] There is pride of *wealth*: "The Son of man hath not where to lay his head."[3] If God has blessed your hand and your household, you must be careful. When God has blessed your gifting and your salary, take care because if you don't stay prayed up and humble, the spirit of pride will get in and cause you to desire things no one else has. It will cause you desire things, not because you want them, but so that you can feel exclusive and superior for having them. If that's your motive, it is totally wrong.

There is nothing wrong with doing things that others haven't done and having things that others don't have. But if your motive is to brag or show others up or to feel superior, that is not the will of God. So, if you have been blessed materially by God, and you desire something, check your motives.

There's pride of *personal appearance*: "He hath no form nor comeliness."[4] This applies to both men and women. In fact, I think that sometimes the women suffer with this form of pride more than men. Especially in church. The church is not a fashion show. No one is exclusive. Jesus showed us that. He looked like a common man. He didn't dress as one would expect a religious teacher to dress.

I often dress in work attire. People don't realize I'm a pastor unless I tell them. I don't walk around every day with a suit on, although I think that is what people expect sometimes. A holy life is lived by the way we act and, in our conversation, not with how we look on the outside.

There is pride of *reputation*: "Made himself of no reputation." Some people want to be known. How many of you get your feelings hurt when you post something on social media, and you only get three likes? And if you get 200 likes you feel great. Our feelings are often based on something out in the land of the internet. Jesus wasn't concerned about His reputation. He didn't have to be. His gifting and calling went before Him. He didn't have to advertise who He was. His life proved it instead.

You don't have to promote yourself. You don't have to advertise that you are a prayer warrior. You don't have to always announce when you pray for someone. You don't need that recognition. The only recognition you need is from God when you serve Him with a humble heart. Jesus resisted the pride of reputation.

There's pride of *superiority*: "I am ... as he that serveth."⁵ I have been a pastor for a long time and I'm getting older and have people working under me. The pride of superiority is a trap I can fall easily into. Often, I want to tell my people what to do, to remind them that I've been doing it a long time and that they can learn a lot from me. Then the Lord reminds me that I don't need to do all that. They already know that I have experience and that I'm the boss. So, the Lord tells me to just go on and let them do the work and that they are qualified and equipped and gifted. This is something that I need to practice in my own life. I need to be like Jesus and resist the pride of superiority.

## CHAPTER FOUR
### *"It's About Jesus"*

*"Let this mind be in you, which was also in Christ Jesus:*

*Who, being in the form of God, thought it not robbery to be equal with God:*

*But made himself of no reputation, and took upon him the form of a servant, and was made in the likeness of men: And being found in fashion as a man, he humbled himself, and became obedient unto death, even the death of the cross."*

—PHILIPPIANS 2:5-8 (KJV)

*"For whether is greater, he that sitteth at meat, or he that serveth? is not he that sitteth at meat? but I am among you as he that serveth."*

—LUKE 22:27 (KJV)

Jesus told His disciples that they had seen the Father when they had seen Him. But at the same time, He was willing to put on an apron and grab a towel and wash their feet. He was there to serve. You will never win anyone to Jesus without a servant's heart. There is no room for the pride of superiority. When we start feeling that way, that is the devil doing his work. And if you step into this sin, God will call you out to serve. He will make you give something up that you love. He will make you do random acts of kindness—in secret.

Do something nice for someone and don't tell anyone about it. That's God's solution to this type of pride. Be like Jesus. Because you will never be a true light to them if you think you are better than them and have everything figured out. Just because you can quote scripture to people doesn't mean a thing if your heart isn't in the right place. They must see the light in you. They must believe you and see something genuine and real in you. When sharing the light of the Lord there is no room for pride.

When God tells you to do a random act of kindness, do it. Without telling anyone. With no reputation. That's humility. Now, the person you did a kind thing for may tell others, and that's ok. The point is that you do something without seeking that recognition.

There is also pride of ability: "I can of mine own self do nothing."[6] Many of us are talented. We have strengths and abilities that others may not have. But we must remember that every good and perfect gift comes from the Lord. I can't be worried about rejection. I can't stress about who wants me and who doesn't want me. Who likes me and who doesn't like me. And if you decide you want someone else, I will be just fine, because God will open another door. Of my own self I can do nothing. And as the Pastor, I am not to be worshiped. It's about the father. Don't lift me up. It's about Jesus. It is about the anointing. It's about the Holy Ghost. And without the gifting of God, I couldn't do what I do. I can do nothing without Him. I would have no voice without Him. I couldn't strike a note without Him. It is all because of Him.

So, we have to make a practice of getting out of the way.

Then there is the pride of *will*. Jesus sought the will of the Father over His own. He wanted to do whatever the Lord told Him to do. And that thought should make us want to go back to the altar and pray.

A man who doesn't profess salvation once offer me money. And it wasn't good money. Did you know that not all money is good money? Sometimes people offer you something that is not the will of the Lord. Sometimes it isn't good. I don't care how much it is. Sometimes more money means less peace, more responsibility, and more sleepless nights. And with more money comes more stewardship. With more money comes the temptation to the spirit of entitlement.

Sometimes when I am meditating, I think I should sell everything. Now, I'm not going to do that, unless the Lord tells me to. But the truth is we don't need so much of what we have. We just want it. It's alright to want things, especially if we use our material blessings to bless others, and as long as we aren't attached to those things more than we desire to do God's will.

Recently, I saw a house in another town and under the carport there was a coffin. A casket. I just had to wonder why it was there? Are you going to throw some of your stuff in there for storage? Why would you want this thing around your house? What kind of person are you? Remind me to say no if you invite me over. I'm trying to understand the mindset of the person who has a casket in their carport. I know I wouldn't want that as a piece of furniture in my house. Sometimes people want all kinds of things, but it's important to be like Jesus and learn to seek out only what God wants for us.

There's pride of *resentment*. When Jesus was on the cross, he prayed forgiveness for those who put Him there. He rejected resentment. Resentment does not feel good. Do you ever get bad vibes when someone comes around? Do you have an unforgiving spirit in you? There are many ways to describe it, and sometimes we want to make it seem less sinful and more acceptable in our lives. But Jesus shows us how to get rid of the spirit of pride when we have been wronged. Even when we feel entitled to revenge. We want to get 'em back. I know that there are some people who should be glad that I'm saved and I know the Lord, because they did me wrong and took my money and everything else. The old me would have retaliated. But today I love Jesus, and I keep going back to the Word, where He shows us with His own life that we are to forgive those who harm us.

In Luke 23:34, Jesus was talking about those that beat Him and crucified Him at Calvary. A lot of those people didn't actually know who He was, but many of them did and they still participated in His death. You would think that would make it harder for Jesus to forgive them. They seemed to know what they were doing. But Jesus knew that if they truly knew exactly what they were doing, they never would have crucified Him.

In our own lives it is hard to forgive those who have hurt us. That cousin or sibling that know exactly what they are doing. They know exactly why they don't want you at their barbecue or in their home. They know exactly why they have your money. They know exactly why they'll take a trip and won't let you in on it. And then they will brag about it on Facebook and let everyone see the great time that they had, so that they can rub it in your face. And you want to call them up and retaliate. But don't. Stay off Facebook and don't participate in all that foolishness. Don't let them know how much it is getting to you. Forgive them and release them. You have a better friend in Jesus than you have with anyone else in the world.

## CHAPTER FIVE
*"There is Only One Road"*

We all struggle with pride. This fact must be accepted and taken to heart. The minute you react with, "not me," is exactly the minute that pride is revealing itself in you. When we think we don't have any issues, and therefore no need to analyze ourselves, that is pride. We are all works in progress. We were all born with Adam's nature. It is human nature to become prideful. And the only solution for that pride is for the Lord to step in.

Now, there is a certain type of pride that is legitimate. But I must tread carefully here, because we all have the capacity for self-deception. You can have confidence and pride in the work God has blessed you to do, as long as you acknowledge that the only reason you were able to do it was Him—because God equips those He calls.

Years ago, I noticed that when I would start projects placed on my heart by the Lord, He would guide my mind, and even my hands. I felt God showing me, teaching me, and accomplishing the task at hand. So, I could be proud of a job well done, but I don't get the glory for it. God does. Because without Him I wouldn't have been able to do it. Without the Lord, I was destined to be a failure in man's eyes. Humility is knowing that not for one moment is any of our success because of us. It's all because of Him.

Pride has so many levels. Pride causes a person to self-inflate and then self-exalt. There is something in you that makes you want to shine for the world to see. You want to be noticed and wanted. This type of pride can be a trap. The purpose of pride is to make you think you are bigger and better than you are, as well as the desire for the world to know just how great you are.

But the Bible says that we should esteem others. That's a job. Your job is to raise up others and not yourself. When we choose pride rather than esteeming others, our blessings get cut off. The recognition we get when we puff ourselves up becomes our only reward, instead of receiving the abundant blessings of God.

Pride is an enemy to God. He hates a proud look, let alone a proud heart. Pride builds a wall between you and God. The spirit of pride is what separates us from the Lord. It is an abomination.

In Leviticus, we learn of some other things that are an abomination. We tend to be quick to point out those sins in others. But if you are quick to point out the abomination in others, and you have a two-by-four in your own eye, you are the one who is struggling with pride. You want to point out a gnat in another's eye, while ignoring the plank in your own. Pride will never let you see the metaphorical plank in your own eye. Pride doesn't want you to be honest with yourself about your own sins and shortcomings.

Pride only wants you to judge others so you feel better about yourself.

Thankfully, God knows your heart. He knows what He has to work with. And the Bible tells us that the heart is desperately wicked. So pride can creep in. Pride will search out your accomplishments and talents and amplify them. Pride will find things that you are good at and try to make them glow. Pride knows what you are capable of. And if it wants you bad enough, it will allow you to do some good and accomplish some things only to tear you down. Because pride also understands what the Word says. The people who exalt themselves will be humbled by God.

However, the person who humbles himself will be exalted by the Lord. So don't worry when you can't exalt yourself. Don't worry when man doesn't recognize your accomplishments. Don't worry when man doesn't choose you. Don't worry when man doesn't put you at the top of the list. Don't worry when man looks at everyone else but you. Don't worry when it seems like your chance will never come. Instead, humble yourself under the mighty hand of God and He will exalt you in due season.

Scripture tells us that pride goes before destruction. Sometimes when we see scandals in different places and ministries, we can see the spirit of pride has caused them to rise to the top. And when they hit the top and plateau and peak, that's when pride turns on them. The exposure and public humiliation—that's what the devil does. He tricks. He builds you up and gives you things, and he makes you think you are really something.

    I remember one time I was celebrating something; I can't even remember what it was. Maybe a birthday. But the people wanted to get a limousine to pick me up. And I said no. I wanted no part of it because I've seen what happens when people get accustomed to being built up like that. I don't want pride to take hold of me. I don't want to play around with my flesh and those feelings and lose my soul.

    I'd rather not take that chance on those kinds of things.

There are some celebrity preachers who started out in the Word, walking in holiness, and teaching about God. I would watch them and think that finally we had someone in the public eye who would preach the truth about Christ to the body of Christ. I would be hopeful. But after a few $50,000 offerings and a few limousine rides from the hotel to the studio and other places, and after writing books and selling CDs, the money started coming in and things changed.

I don't want money or material things to change me. That's not to say that we can't long for material things and financial security. But I don't want money, or things, or connections, or status to change me. The Bible says that God would put us among great men. There is nothing wrong with that. But if that causes you to not be able to pray or fast like you used to, or if it changes you and you no longer want to come to the altar and repent before the Lord, and you find other routes in the Word of God that excuse you, then something is wrong.

When I am driving and need directions to my destination, sometimes I use different GPS systems. Sometimes I use Apple maps. Sometimes Google maps. Sometimes I look at both to see which is faster, because they tend to take different routes to get there. But they both get me to the destination eventually.

The Word of God cannot be just an option to take. If you don't like it, you can choose another route. You see, there is no reroute through the scriptures. There is only one road. Anything outside of that route is simply pride.

The life of Christ rebuked pride. His life exemplified humility, even though He was God. The Bible tells us that He humbled Himself, even to the death on the cross. Because He knew that pride leads to destruction.

Pride leads to shame. "When pride cometh, then cometh shame: but with the lowly is wisdom." (Proverbs 11:2)

Pride leads to arguments. "Only by pride cometh contention: but with the well advised is wisdom." (Proverbs 13:10) In any household or job or game, a person will be more successful if they humble themselves and don't try to do it all on their own and get all the glory for themselves.

LeBron James is not one of my favorite celebrities. But he is talented. And he didn't get to where he is by hogging the ball. No. He can pass the ball and let someone else score some points. A real team player will include his teammates. A prideful person will only care about how many points he can get and how famous he can become. "I hit the last three point shot". They got me on camera." And eventually that will catch up with them. They will be pulled out of the game.

Humility has a way of putting us in our place.

We can choose humility instead of having to be humiliated because our pride caused us to fall. If you humble yourself, God will raise you up to where you need to be. But the reason people miss their calling, the reason they miss their mark, is pride. Pride decides we should bless ourselves, because we do not want to wait for God's plan and His timing.

We think we deserve more, and we deserve it now.

## CHAPTER SIX
### *"Check My Heart, Lord"*

Pride will be punished. "Every one that is proud in heart is an abomination to the Lord: though hand join in hand, he shall not be unpunished." (Proverbs 16:5) God hates pride. It will be punished. I would hate for the Lord to allow me to preach and love the people in my own way and do what is right in my own eyes, only to stand before the judgment seat of Christ and be told that I can't come in. Because I did what I did with the heart of iniquity. I did it with the spirit of pride. I looked down on others and exalted myself above everyone. And that is not what the Lord told me to do. He told me to exalt others rather than self. So when I stand before the Lord, I don't want Him to write off everything I have done.

And what if, after this happened, I see people that I knew on earth that I preached to entering the kingdom. But why, God? I preached the word to those people. I got them out of the world and into the house of the Lord. Why do they get to enter and not me? And the Lord tells me that, yes, I did all of that, but I did it with the wrong spirit. I did it in the spirit of pride, which the Lord hates. What if God told me that He watched me preach and He hated the spirit of pride in which I preached. Even though I gave, and even double tithed, I did it in a spirit that looked down on others. Those that I witnessed to will make it in, but the Lord was watching me while I witnessed to them, and He hated what He saw. The people I preached to would get a seat in the kingdom, but I have to depart from Him. Because the spirit in which I did things for the Lord was not approved by Him.

Jesus came in a lowly way. You know the Christmas story. He was born stable and laid in a cattle trough because there was no room for Him. Jesus said, "Come unto me, all ye that labour and are heavy laden, and I will give you rest. Take my yoke upon you, and learn of me; for I am meek and lowly in heart: and ye shall find rest unto your souls." Jesus was meek and lowly in heart. I want to humble myself like Jesus. I don't want God to humble me. I don't want to wait until something happens in my life that makes me pray. I don't want to wait for destruction before I turn to Him. That is a tedious journey.

I think that a lot of people are going to be surprised. The things we do in His name are often done by exalting ourselves. And Jesus hates that.

Pride ends in destruction. "Pride goeth before destruction, and an haughty spirit before a fall." (Proverbs 16:18) There is no place for proud boasting in the life of a child of God. And we have to watch our words. We can be sarcastic, or say things that we don't even really mean, and they may be taken as pride from someone else and those words may cause them to stumble.

Remember when we were first saved? We watched everything we did and everything we said. We wanted to please God so much and we were very careful. But after a few black eyes from the enemy, and then after a few blessings of the Lord, we thought we were okay. I must be doing just fine. God is blessing me. He's providing. It looks like I'm winning over the devil. Pride sets in.

Check my heart, Lord. Before you have to check my pulse, check my heart. Show me the things that have caused it to be clogged. Show me personalities, wrong spirits in me, that have clogged up my heart for you. Lord, check me for resentments and unforgiveness, which shows pride. "I don't need to forgive them. I don't need anyone."

No one can force this heart check on you. You must go to the throne for yourself and allow the Lord to pull those things out. I would much rather go to the Lord on my own and deal with my pride and sin privately than have Him pull everything out and expose me to others. Let's just make it right, Jesus. Let me be willing to have the Lord search my heart. I hope there is nothing there that He hates, but if there is, reveal it to me and take it away. I don't want it there. I don't want to be like that.

Some preachers are not sensitive enough to realize that sometimes you must leave the 99 and go after that one. When a church member is deceived and leaves, we must go after that one because we will stand before God and answer to Him for how we handled losing the one. Maybe there was a misunderstanding. We must humble ourselves to make things right if there is a spirit of pride in us. To admit we can be wrong and make it right.

But instead, preachers think, "Well, they have the Holy Ghost, so they are supposed to know what I meant. I don't have to go after them. I don't need to humble myself."

And if the spirit of the Lord has led them somewhere else, I can't be blamed for that. I can't change that. It's happened time and time again. People are dealing with issues and sin and when I preach on something they take it personally, even though I had no idea what they were dealing with. And they start thinking that I must know something and that I'm preaching at them. And so, they leave. Well, I can't help that person. They weren't willing to humble themselves and come and have a conversation with me. All they had to do was come to me and tell me that they were feeling convicted. Any of that would stay between them, me and the Lord. And we would have the opportunity to clear up any misunderstanding and make things right. But they don't want to do that.

We must speak on the issues in our lives. We must voice our pride. When we don't, when we stuff it down and avoid dealing with it, we suffer. We need to get on our knees or even our face before the Lord and cry to God because there is an enemy that doesn't want that to happen. Satan doesn't want our secrets and sins to be brought to the light. He doesn't want us to reveal the truth. But the Lord reveals Himself to the humble, not the proud.

## CHAPTER SEVEN
### *"Holier than Thou"*

---

*"For ye see your calling, brethren, how that not many wise men after the flesh, not many mighty, not many noble, are called: But God hath chosen the foolish things of the world to confound the wise; and God hath chosen the weak things of the world to confound the things which are mighty; And base things of the world, and things which are despised, hath God chosen, yea, and things which are not, to bring to nought things that are: That no flesh should glory in his presence. But of him are ye in Christ Jesus, who of God is made unto us wisdom, and righteousness, and sanctification, and redemption: That, according as it is written, He that glorieth, let him glory in the Lord."*

—I CORINTHIANS 1:26-31

God resists the proud. But He reveals Himself to the humble. Do you want to see things of the Lord? Do you want to have visions and dreams? Do you want God to give you revelations?

Then let Him know how bad you need Him and let Him know that you can't make it without Him. Humble yourself under the mighty hand of God. Believe that the little, unseen things that you do for the Lord matter. When you are humble, you are not a flattery magnet. When you are humble, you don't need to feed off compliments from others. A flattery magnet has an appetite for flattery and compliments. And the more you get, the more that appetite grows. So, you spend more time with people who will flatter you, and the cycle grows.

Humility does not desire that. When we are humble, we care about what God thinks and we surround ourselves that will speak truth to us, telling us who we are and who we are not. We don't only want to hear the good stuff. We also are open to hearing about what needs to be changed in us.

Tell me that I need to get a haircut. Tell me that I have something between my teeth. Tell me when I waxed the car that I missed a spot. And if people tell you those things, don't get offended.

I spent time with Bishop Rick August, and I noticed that he is not a person that you can flatter. He does not pay any attention to flattery or compliments only for the purpose of manipulation. That stuff isn't important to him. He knows there is no need for that because we only need to know that

God approves of us, not someone else. We don't need to wait on man to build us up. When we are built up by man, we open ourselves up to being manipulated and deceived, all in the form of flattery. And we open ourselves to the spirit of pride. It's a terrible spirit and a twisting spirit that will tangle you up and create problems.

Sometimes God will say, "I'm going to break you so that you learn to love me and everything and everyone else around you. Because right now your perspective and your motives are twisted by pride."

> *"But he giveth more grace. Wherefore he saith, God resisteth the proud, but giveth grace unto the humble."*
>
> —JAMES 4:6

Pride cuts us off from God and others.

> *"And he spake this parable unto certain which trusted in themselves that they were righteous, and despised others: Two men went up into the temple to pray; the one a Pharisee, and the other a publican. The Pharisee stood and prayed thus with himself, God, I thank thee, that I am not as other men are, extortioners, unjust, adulterers, or even as this publican. I fast twice in the week, I give tithes of all that I possess. And the publican, standing afar off, would not lift up so much as his eyes unto heaven, but smote upon his breast, saying, God be merciful to me a sinner. I tell you, this man went down to his*

> *house justified rather than the other: for every one that exalteth himself shall be abased; and he that humbleth himself shall be exalted."*

—LUKE 18:9-14

That is a parable of Jesus. Two men went to the temple to do the same thing. To pray. One was a Pharisee, and one was a publican, or a tax collector. (The tax collectors usually did not know the Lord and were known for their greed and corruption, only seeking money and wealth.)

And there are people in churches today like them. People who think that the act of going to church is what keeps you right with God. They go to church, thinking they are alright, and when they are dismissed go and do whatever they want to do. But the church building doesn't save you. It's what you allow in and out of your heart. The evil goes out and the glory comes in. The love of God comes in and you are baptized the right way.

So, these two men went to the temple to pray. The Pharisees were a judgmental group of religious leaders. They literally thought they were holier than thou. They prided themselves on upholding the law and they did not appreciate Jesus, or the radical things He was teaching. They watched Jesus and were waiting for Him to make a mistake so they could accuse Him of breaking the law. They knew the law, and they followed the law but only on the outside. For the praise and recognition of others. They would fast and then walk around looking hungry and disfiguring their faces so everyone would know how righteous they were. They were looking for rewards from men. Don't be like that.

So, the Pharisee stood, separate from the sinful publican, and prayed for all to hear. He started naming the sins of the publican, thanking God that he wasn't like that sinner. I kind of think that when he said that, he glared over at the publican. He went on to brag about all the righteous things he did. He paid tithes on everything he possessed, he went above and beyond the requirement and fasted twice per week.

I do this. I do that. I. I. I. The letter I is in the word sin and the word pride. We must make sure that we don't fall into this trap. Taking credit for things that belong to the Lord. I built the church. I built the fellowship hall. I donated this or that. I picked out the church van.

The word High also has the letter I. Mount Everest is the highest point you can reach in the world. So many people want to climb it and attempt to climb it. But the higher up the mountain that you go, the lower the oxygen level becomes. Many have died trying to reach the pinnacle because they were trying to get too high.

So, the Pharisee was praying all the way up in the front of the temple. Up by the oil, and the basin where you wash. He felt like he was worthy. He washed his clothes and his hands and walked right to the front. He thought he was all that. He thought he was so holy that he would shake the heavens with his prayer.

But the publican did not feel worthy. He stayed in the back. And God heard Him. (You better be careful about talking bad about people who sit in that back, because God just might be ready to do something for them.) And the publican fell to the ground because he did not believe that he deserved to stand before a holy God. He didn't approach God with pride, but with complete humility, knowing that without God he was nothing. All that he had achieved didn't mean anything when he was before God.

Unlike the pharisee, he knew that the only way we are going to shake the heavens is through revival. I watched a documentary on AA Allen, the famous evangelist. They would fill tents with thousands of people. A woman came forward who had a tumor in her belly. It was a very large tumor, very visible to anyone looking at her. And while he was praying for her, he hit her and BOOM. God healed her and the tumor dissolved right away. Her dress even fell off because the swelling in her stomach went down, because she was dressing to cover the tumor. But she had a slip on, and the ladies swarmed her to get her covered back up.

These were praying folk. They would have a tent meeting and have three services per day. And now we can hardly get anyone for three hours a week.

I remember when Brother Sam Sallis, an evangelist from Midland, Pennsylvania, who had a tent revival. He had healing lines and the holy ghost was moving. Folks were getting saved for real! I'm so glad that I got saved for real. And not this microwave stuff going on right now. Too many people think they got it when they haven't done anything. You must come to an altar and repent. You must get in some water. You must give up something. You can't just assume that God is okay with you. You must die to self and let Him resurrect you. That's what the baptism is all about. The watery grave.

And the publican had a sincere desire to be saved by God. He couldn't even lift his eyes up to heaven because he knew he was unworthy. But he desired mercy. When you go to God in this manner, it should be so powerful that you cry. Please God have mercy on me. I don't even deserve the strength to be on my knees before you. I have too much baggage in my life. And I'm still a sinner. I haven't gotten rid of all my bad habits and struggles yet. Jesus, help me. Because I know that

I'm covered under the blood. We should come before Him as an empty pitcher before a full fountain, that is, Jesus.

In contrast, the Pharisee was coming like he knew the Almighty Jehovah. As if he was Solomon, thanking God that he wasn't like other sinners. Thanking God and presuming that He accepted his praise and worship. Assuming that God has his name written on a seat in heaven. That wasn't thanks. That was pride.

The scripture say the righteous would scarcely make it in. But the publican humbled himself. And he may have heard the Pharisee praying about him. But he didn't respond. You must come to the place where you never criticize the person that is criticizing you. Don't put down the one that's trying to show you up. Don't retaliate. Let them get their earthly recognition and glory.

Let God take care of the rest.

## CHAPTER EIGHT
*"He is God, and We Are Not"*

Many of us struggle with saying we are sorry. We don't want to apologize. That's pride. People covet and want to have what others have. That's also rooted in pride. You see, pride leads to self-deception and other forms of evil. If you want to read more on that, check out Galatians 6:3, Deuteronomy 8:17-18, Isaiah 16:6, or Jeremiah 49:16.

Pride causes spiritual blindness. When a person is full of pride, it causes the spirit of blindness because they can't see anything except themselves. Their perspective. Their desires. Their entitlements. They can't see what God wants them to see. Pride will shut you off to where God won't trust you with what He wants for you. God won't show you anything. You won't dream about spiritual things. The only thing you will see and believe are the lies that you tell yourself. Pride causes us to make up things, and project things onto God that aren't from Him.

Pride causes people to give themselves position and authority, pretending that they have heard from God. Yet God isn't even talking to them because they are full of pride. If we are full of pride, we won't hear His voice. God won't use us if we are full of pride.

Pride is dangerous. It is a weapon of mass destruction, causing spiritual blindness. Jeremiah 43:2, Nehemiah 9:16.

Pride causes a hard heart. Sometimes people can challenge us. What we need in these situations is a tough skin and a soft heart. But pride gets in the way. And it causes us to have soft skin and a hard heart. We must pray about that. When we have soft skin and a hard heart we are easily offended. And that causes our hearts to harden even more. But if we have a tough hide, or a hardened skin, those things that could offend you won't be able to penetrate, and your heart will stay soft.

For more about what the Bible has to say about pride causing a hard heart, you can read Psalm 36:2, 10:3, 52:1; Daniel 5:20.

Pride causes a malicious spirit. We read about this in Psalm 119:85, 73:8, 140:5.

Pride causes contempt for others. Psalms 123:4, 119:51 and Proverbs 21:24.

Pride causes quarreling or arguments. Proverbs 13:10.

Pride causes violence. Psalm 73:6, 86:14. Esther 3:5-6.

Do you remember the story of David and Goliath? David walked in humility. Goliath was full of pride. Goliath knew how big and powerful he was and assumed that he would have the victory. But the Lord was with David.

When you walk in humility the Lord is with you. When you walk in pride you will be fighting on your own with only your own strength. The enemy is a big bully, and we can't defeat him in our own power and strength. Humility gives us the spirit of the Lord, so we can fight the enemy with His power and strength.

Pride causes injustice. Psalm 119:78, 56:2. This is easy for us to understand because of the racial tension that we have seen throughout the country and the world. Groups promoting White power, Black power, and any other organization driven by hatred. So be careful about supporting something that sounds good on the outside, but we don't really know their hearts.

You must be wise and follow God. Follow the Word of God. Don't chase after other things. One of the most dangerous things about pride, and how people can be blinded because of it, is because the devil takes something that has some truth in it, but then twists it and warps it into something evil. It is like the danger or other religions. There is some truth in other religions and denominations. There are good spiritual practices, but the foundation is wrong. And that's why people fall. They want to read out of their own Bible that was written for them and what they believe. They don't want to use your Bible. There is a little bit of truth in Islam. And that's where the danger comes in.

There's a danger in pride when it comes to success and accomplishments. People attach the word *favor* to it. They make it seem like they are extra special to God because of their success. God has special favor for them, based on how good they are.

Pride can be accompanied by temporary prosperity. Psalm 73:3, 10:5. I can have prosperity in the world's eyes by getting something that the Lord didn't direct me to get, or getting involved in something that the Lord didn't tell me to get involved in. Just going off on my own and doing what I think is best for me. And at first, we may call that favor, but eventually it becomes a burden. And eventually we must let it go, which is hard because we think we deserve everything. And we see prosperity as favor, when sometimes it is our failure. That's why we must pray. That's why we must listen to the Holy Ghost. Psalms 73:3, 10:5.

Pride ends in disaster. Proverbs 16:5. The New Living Translation reads, "The Lord detests the proud; they will surely be punished." When proud people are around you, that doesn't mean that we are happy that they will be punished. But just trust God that He will take care of that, and we don't have to. Sometimes we think God is taking to long to punish those who have hurt us. Sometimes it seems like others are getting away with a whole lot of sin and evil. But that's none of our business. That is up to God. He is God and we are not.

And we should never rejoice when our enemy falls. Because that is pride. If someone hurts you, never rejoice when they fall. Pray for them. Don't criticize them. You will never criticize the person that you truthfully pray for.

Doctors seem to know how pride fits into human thinking. Perhaps there is a good reason why pride is considered one of the seven deadly sins. We've all been repelled by people who have an inflated view of themselves. You know you are thinking of someone right now. But the underlying problem is not that they don't think much of themselves. They have low self-esteem, and they are insecure. So, they must inflate and promote themselves to others.

There is a particular type of fish that blows himself up to try to intimidate another fish. He blows himself up to intimidate the enemy. He swells up his mouth to make himself look bigger than he knows he is. That is a good analogy for pride. Self-inflating to look bigger than we are.

Self-inflating to look like we wish we could be. It is a person who operates in a false self.

This generation that we are in today, and especially young people, face a lot of false information. Not a lot of truth. And it causes self-inflation to be the norm. It's all about me. My truth. And it's so easy to see. I'm not being judgmental, but it is simply true that a tree shall be known by its fruit. You can just see it. The outward appearance is so made up and perfect, and they are projecting a perfect life on social media and in public. And they look so proud. But really, they are just self-inflated.

God does not want His church to be this way. We will never receive from God if we care more about what our life looks like to others than to Him. And this self-inflated view is easy to spot in other people. When people talk about themselves excessively and rarely show interest in others. A proud person is never a soul winner. It's all about them. A proud person will never draw anyone closer to the Lord. They don't want to be bothered.

I'm so thankful that someone was bothered enough to take time to lead me closer to the Lord. Someone called me and invited me. And after I came to the Lord, someone checked on me. But proud people go to church to feel better, to get their hit from the church, and then go home and don't think about anyone else. Because pride won't let you reach out to a person for their benefit and throw a life raft to a drowning man.

Pride will always want you to look bigger and taller and better in life than anyone else, to the point where you will not be interested in helping anyone but yourself. You want to look big. You want to consume. You want people to see how many degrees you have so they can think you are important. We shouldn't have to tell people how great we are. If we are truly great, we will stay humble, and people will figure it out on their own.

In fact, pride can turn people away. It can keep you from getting certain jobs. People can see through it and know that you aren't a team player. Or maybe you inflate yourself on your resume so much that they don't offer you the job because they decide they can't afford you. So, they don't even call you. That happened to me once when I was looking for job. I told them all my qualifications and capabilities and schooling and work history, and they looked at me and told me they only hired tractor hands there. And they told me to have a nice day. I oversold myself and overqualified myself right out of a job opportunity that I needed.

Even though I didn't mean to, maybe they were afraid that I would make more money than them. Maybe they thought that I thought I was better than them. Maybe they were intimidated. So, they would rather just pass than have to hang around with someone like that.

And there is a personality that should be reflected by the Jesus in you. We should not even have the appearance of looking down on someone. Or talking down to someone. We shouldn't try to make ourselves to be bigger than we are. Overconfidence and arrogance push us away. We should check our pride level. According to the Word of God and according to others around me. If it seems like no one wants to be around me and I have no friends, something is wrong. God put us on this planet to live in community with others. We are supposed to be able to get along. To appreciate each other's differences. We don't all have to be the same and think the same and accomplish the same. We may not all look alike.

Maybe weight issues run in the family and it's hereditary and it's extremely hard to get rid of it. So, if I don't want to be this way as generations before me were, then I need to eat differently than they ate. I need to change my diet. I need to move more, so I don't end up with health issues. I'm going to be different. But it doesn't mean I'm doing it out of pride or that I am judging them. I'm not going to have overconfidence and arrogance about it that pushes people away. I still relate to them as equals. They don't think that I think I'm better than they are. People appreciate you when you appreciate them and respect them.

# CHAPTER NINE
## *"We Don't Have to Know Everything"*

A while back I invited a man to church, and he visited. He was sitting in the back. I found out that he didn't have a home. He was living in an old building. So, I went by there and saw that he was living in a building that he bought, and he also had a brand new truck. He was making do and making happen what needed to happen. I didn't have to get into his business and feel sorry for him and feel better than him. Pride can cause us to be nosy when we think we are doing better than someone else.

The devil is sneaky, and he wants us to feel inflated around others. So, we must relate to others as equals, instead of delivering an aura of obnoxious superiority that makes people feel small.

I know a guy who works a job and owns another business. And some people call him big money, and easy money. But none of that is true. They don't know where he used to work and the hard work he did and the sacrifices he made and the money he saved to get to where he is now. It wasn't easy. And maybe he was still paying off notes and other insurance bills. Just because it looks like easy money on the outside does not mean that is accurate. And we don't have to assume that he thinks he's better than everyone just because he has a business. He struggles just like the rest of us. We are equals. Money shouldn't impress or intimidate us.

Pride is often driven by poor self-worth and shame. Prideful people need recognition and affirmation from others to feel good about themselves.

It's a mindset. Pride is often driven by poor self-worth or poor self-esteem. They don't think they are good enough. So, they must blow themselves up to look bigger than they feel. You feel badly about yourself. So, you overcompensate with a false sense of superiority. But deep down you have so much fear and don't like yourself very much.

Have you ever met a narcissist? A narcissist is really a child in an adult body. A spoiled brat that is hiding what they really feel. They must constantly put others down and act tough and mean, but deep down they are hurting and scared.

When people act out, it's often because they are afraid. They hide that fear by snapping and going off on others. They get loud and they scream. And sometimes the police must get involved because maybe they get violent. But deep down, they are a child on the inside. A child that is ashamed and fearful. Shame drives pride.

The person who never knew where to get money and never lived in a decent place must blow himself up to appear prosperous. But it's a false bravado. Just go to work and pay your bills. Everything will be okay. You don't have to brag about anything. You don't have to tell people how well you are doing. You don't have to show the world that your house is decorated better than other houses. It's ok to have nice things, but you don't have to go out of your way to show people all your nice things so you can feel good about yourself. That desire is driven by a lack of self-worth. You feel so bad about yourself that you compensate that bad feeling by feeling superior based on what you have.

And not only do we compensate by blowing ourselves up, but we purposely look for other people's flaws so we can feel superior at their expense. When we focus on and talk about other people's flaws, it allows us to ignore our own. When there is something wrong with everyone else but me, pride is the culprit.

Have you ever been around someone like that? Someone who has a negative word to say about everyone. They never have anything good to say. Deep down, that is a hurting, wounded person who had been broken and crushed by life. And the only way they know how to express themselves is by talking down about someone else. Because it makes them feel superior and better about themselves.

Proverbs 6:16-19 says, 6:16 "These six things doth the LORD hate: yea, seven are an abomination unto him: A proud look, a lying tongue, and hands that shed innocent blood, An heart that deviseth wicked imaginations, feet that be swift in running to mischief, A false witness that speaketh lies, and he that soweth discord among brethren."

All these things that the Lord hates stem from pride. Think back to your school days. If there was a fight, we all ran to see who was going to win. It's a fight, it's a fight! The whole crowd runs toward it and gathers around it. We were swift to run to mischief.

Proverbs 6:16-19 tells us the deadly sins and they all stem from pride.

Pride prevents us from acknowledging our human vulnerabilities. I will be the first to tell you that I don't know something. Maybe you will think that makes me look stupid. I don't care. Because I know that it is better to know our weaknesses and limits than to pretend that we know everything to make ourselves look better. And just because I don't know how to do a particular thing, doesn't mean I can't do others. It's not a measure of my intelligence or worth.

But pride keeps us from showing our vulnerabilities because we don't want to look weak or stupid, and we don't want others to seem better than us.

We don't have to know everything. We don't have to be good at everything. We are all good at some things. We all know some things. It's not a contest. It's ok to show vulnerability. And when you realize that you will not worry when someone knows how to do something that you don't know how to do. You don't have to worry that they are better than you.

Believe me when I say there are certain things that you wouldn't want me to do. You don't want me driving an 18-wheeler or a fancy log truck. Nope. I will just stick with what I know.

Be glad that you know what you know. Thank God for your calling and giftings. Don't worry about what you don't have compared to others. Don't allow others to make you feel stupid. God created us all differently and for a purpose. He loves us too much to give us all the same things.

I tried to learn how to French braid my little girl's hair once. It didn't pan out. So, I had to admit that I had no clue

## REBUKING THE SPIRIT OF PRIDE

of how to make it happen. I tried, and I failed. But I didn't feel stupid or less than who I was.

Shame-driven pride makes us too uncomfortable to say, "I'm sorry, I was wrong, I made a mistake, and I don`t know." When pride rules, we believe we're always right. This makes it difficult to sustain intimate relationships; nobody likes being with a know-it-all.

When I was younger, I had a friend that was so arrogant and would never apologize. And it made me not want to be around them.

Today, I may not always have it all together, and I'm a work in progress. But if I hurt you, I will apologize to you.

Pride doesn't want you to apologize and admit you are wrong. And pride will always keep you feeling like you are owed an apology. That's why in a home, or in a relationship, you must humble yourselves. Otherwise, the fight will never end. Someone must choose humility to actually be the bigger person and say I'm sorry. It doesn't make you less of a person. Quite the opposite, in fact.

But you must mean it. The apology must be sincere. And pride tells us that we are always right. Humility helps us to take a step back and want peace more than we want to be right.

All of us know someone who always want to be right. That's because pride is ruling this person and it makes it difficult to remain friends. No one likes a know-it-all. But pride will try to get you to prove how good you are and how much you know. And yet it is driven by a fear of how much you are limited and how much you don't know. And you overcompensate to make people believe that you are better than you feel.

As the light of our dignity shines more brightly, we realize that we don't have to be perfect. Showing vulnerability and humility invites people toward us. We become approachable rather than intimidating. We don't see ourselves as better or worse than anyone else. We recognize that we're all a part of the human condition; we all have strengths and weaknesses.

I believe I am anointed by God to preach the Word, but I am so glad that I know I am not perfect, and I don't have to be. I can be myself. People want to see the real me, not someone who tries to prove that I'm better than I am. I want to be down to earth. I don't always wear a suit. I wear tennis shoes like everyone else. I don't pretend to be something I'm not just because I'm a pastor.

It is God's desire that we be ourselves and not imitate others. If we follow God's will for our life, we will never have to apologize for being ourselves. If one would only live a life that pleases God, there would never have to be a front to cover you. God, help us to live in humility and please you.

It is freeing to hold ourselves with the dignity that comes from simply being human. We don't need to achieve "greatness" to have worth and value. We're great just as we are. We might be inclined to pursue excellence because it feels meaningful, enlivening, and expansive, but not because it defines who we are as a person.

## CHAPTER TEN
### *"We Can Rest in His Assurance"*

Some of us have counseled people. Maybe it is your career. Maybe you run a business. Maybe you are in the medical field. Maybe you are a parent. Maybe you work in ministry. At some point we might have to give counsel to someone else.

If you know anything about counseling, there is a first step in getting the process started First, the person who is being counseled must admit that there is a problem that they need help with. Now this is easier said than done. Many of us prefer to live in denial and pretend like we are okay.

I tend to tell people a lot about my life. The good, the bad, and the ugly. My life is an open book before the Lord. But in this world, people are often intoxicated with what others think of them. There is a whole mindset that is centered about how people perceive you. How people view you. It keeps us from being open with others and the Lord. This is serious business. There are some critical things that we must realize. It's not something that can be brushed over. It is something as critical as having to be on dialysis for blood cleansing.

Our life must be cleansed of pride by submitting to the will of God and respecting one another.

It's something that the Lord has dealt with me in my own life. He makes sure that before I try to tell someone else how to live, I make sure that I am practicing what I'm preaching. The message of pride is not a popular journey. Many don't want to hear it. And as I teach on this, adversity after adversity, and challenge after challenge seems to come my way. The enemy doesn't want this subject brought to light. This teaching stirs up the spirits. It's common to encounter things that try to distract us spiritually. Anything to keep us from absorbing the truth that God is leading us to.

We want to be closer to the Lord. But there is a dividing line between us and God. That line is sin. Disobedience that builds a wall between us and God. And the one that builds that wall the highest is the sin of pride. Our motives. I'm so glad that God is teaching me about this, because without it, I can live in denial, unaware and ignorant of the sin that will cause me to live without the favor of God on my life.

Sometimes I have prayed for people who said they have low self-esteem. I am starting to understand that low self-esteem can be a form of pride. When you have low self-esteem, you put yourself in a position of vulnerability. You think you are not as good as others. And you will do things and say things to cover up how you really feel about you. You compare yourself to others. So, you make choices based on the wrong motive.

You are feeling bad about yourself, so you decide to go to the store. Maybe some retail therapy will make you feel better about yourself. Perhaps you change the way you look on the outside to hide and ignore how you feel on the inside. Denial; cover up your feelings and dress them up on the outside. Pride tells me to ignore the negative thoughts and go shopping to make myself feel differently, so others will think I'm doing okay. Pride says, never show your wounds, never let people know things that have really hurt. It's the wrong motive and it is intoxicating. Your whole life is centered around how you seem on the outside and what people think of you.

But your life shouldn't be centered around others' perception of you. Your life needs to be centered on what the Lord thinks about you. How does God look at you? What does He see when He looks at you. What is His perception of you. Is God interested in blessing you? Are you honoring Him with your life? Are you true to the word of God? Are you faithful to His calling on your life? Or are you functioning as a robot in front of people, just going through the motions. Looking like you are okay on the outside.

The only way we can determine this is in the prayer room. Because in the prayer room it is only you and God. You can't impress Him in the same ways that you try to impress and manipulate the perspective of people. He's not impressed by those things. The only thing that impresses Him is our humility and our desire for Him.

Scripture even tells us that people will come to God saying, "Didn't we cast out devils in your name?" But God will say that He never knew them. And He will say, "Depart from me." He's not impressed with our actions when they are motivated by pride. He wants the heart, and you can't fool Him. He desires a relationship with you in the spirit.

And when we do have a true relationship with Him in the spirit we can relax. I can be who I am in God. Jesus accepts me the way I am. I don't have to prove anything to anyone else. We can rest in His assurance.

In Matthew 23, Jesus condemns the Pharisees for being hypocrites. They said one thing but did another. They did this so that they would look good in the eyes of people. This passage makes me look at myself and ask God to examine why I do what I do. Am I doing it for a response from people? Or for a response from God? You see, the pharisees would fast and disfigure their faces to show the world that they were fasting and therefore holy. That was the reward that they were looking for.

But I know that when I pray in secret, God rewards openly. Jesus told us not to do alms before men to be seen of them. If you do something for someone and then boast about it, that is the only reward you will get.

The Pharisees loved attention and they loved that respect and adoration that they received for their positions. I see that in many ministries today, in preachers, pastors, bishops and other church leaders. I've often said that the pulpit is a dangerous place. It is very easy to slip into a place where you are preaching for a response from the crowd. People are shouting back at you, shouting "amen", telling you to keep preaching. It is easy to get comfortable, thinking that you are the one who is doing something. But really it is between me and God, whether someone shouts a hallelujah or glory. Even if the crowd doesn't respond, I can know that I am pleasing Him, if I'm doing it for the right reasons.

There is nothing wrong with appreciating being well spoken of by other people if your motive is pure. If you do good things with the right motives, you will most likely get positive results. But you need to stay humble and just give the glory to God. And if you are preaching the word, if people come back that's a pretty good indicator of whether you are being a blessing to others, no matter if they say it out loud or not. You don't have to wonder if you are getting through to them. The Lord is working in you, and you can give all glory and credit to Him. It is His word that you are teaching, not your own. You didn't write it. They are His rules and laws. And you should love Him for it.

But the Pharisees sought attention and respect, without a genuine desire to help other people or a genuine love for the Lord. They didn't really love God. They didn't really love the people. They just wanted to look good. So, they did things religiously to make themselves look important and holy. They loved standing in the marketplace with their scrolls, wearing their long, ornate robes, so everyone could see them. People thought that they were close to God.

But they were far from God. What was coming out of their mouths was not lining up with the condition of their hearts. You see, when we lift ourselves up in pride, what comes out of our mouths never reflects the true state of our hearts, because our heart motive is to impress, not to serve. Pride makes us say what we don't mean and mean what we don't say. Pride makes us liars.

All of us have been around an outspoken person. Someone asks them a question, and even if they don't know the answer, they make something up that sounds good. You may ask them, "How do you remove an ulcer from a person's stomach?" And they start rambling on about giving them anesthetic and giving them a topical numbing agent before shooting the anesthetic in, and then cleaning the area and using a disinfectant. Then taking the scalpel and understanding where to cut, opening the "gastric intestinal cavity" ......blah blah blah.

Speaking about medical conditions without any training or true knowledge of that field. They are just using big words to sound like they know something. But, they don't have a clue. Yet they keep going to impress you and to make themselves look smart.

That is pride. Pretending that you know something because you don't want to admit that you don't know, or you aren't skilled. That's what the Pharisees would do. They were filled with pride. And if we are not careful, we can turn into modern day Pharisees, acting as if we are above others. That is one of the hallmarks of pride; thinking that you are above others.

## CHAPTER ELEVEN
*"Which One Will You Choose?"*

The first step to defeating pride is admitting what you don't know. Admitting that you don't have all the answers. Admitting that you may need help sometimes.

I have no problem getting out of the way and letting someone else help me. I have no problem admitting that I can't do it all. I can get out of the way. Otherwise, I will spend my time doing things, because I want people to see me working hard, but really I won't be impressing God at all. God doesn't speak to you if you are worried about how you look on the outside. Trying to pretend that you know everything and can do everything yourself. That spirit of pride will keep your prayers from being heard by God. Your prayers will be blocked, and it will separate you from God.

I can't act like I am better than my wife. I can't act like I'm better than my children. I can't act like I'm better than the congregation that I serve. The title of Pastor does not allow me to lord over those that I am supposed to be serving. I don't go around saying, "I'm the pastor," so people recognize how important I am. They already know I'm the pastor.

If we are not careful, we as pastors can turn the pulpit into a dangerous place.

In pride, sometimes people don't know who they really are, and in that weakness, they must promote themselves. They need someone to know who they are. And if you don't know who you are, don't look to others for the answer. Don't become intoxicated by what others think. That's pride.

Instead, we must genuinely love people. We must unconditionally love people. Not just when it suits us, or when it will turn out in our favor.

Ridding ourselves of pride is a process. It won't happen overnight. You've been conditioned all your life to think a certain way. You have a sin nature that has shaped your core beliefs of who you are, and how you relate to yourself and others. That lens of pride is not going to change overnight. Your pride can feel comfortable. Change will feel unnatural and uncomfortable.

People don't like having their pride exposed. They might become offended and could retaliate. The church is a safe place to confront our pride. From a leadership standpoint, having our pride gently pointed out by those who love the

Lord and love you is the safest and best way to start the process of working it out of you. When you see someone that is overtaken in a fault, restore such a person in the spirit of lowliness. Not by lording over them and beating them over the head with a club. You don't have to be negative towards them. You can do it with gentleness and love and grace. Have a spirit of restoration and grace and mercy in your heart, showing them that God loves them and can change them and bring them back to a place of communion and fellowship with Him. Pray that they come to a place of repentance, without gossiping about them. Do it all with a humble heart, knowing that pride can creep up in you if you start believing that you are better than them.

There are only two ways we can be rid of pride. First, we can humbly do it ourselves. Or second, God can break our pride. We can either choose humility, or God will humble us, sometimes through humiliation. Which one will you choose?

I choose humility. I don't want to get to the point that the Lord must break my pride.

I was recently leading a devotion with some people and a lady in the group spoke up and said that she wanted God to humble her. And when it was my turn to speak, I turned to her and humbly told her, "You don't want God to humble you. You want to humble yourself under the mighty hand of God."

I don't want God to break me. I want to realize my brokenness and go to the altar. I want to lay before the Lord in my weakness and cry out to Him and ask Him to shine the light on me, so I can see my faults and pride. I would rather Him shine the light on me in private, than breaking me and shining the light on all my faults for the world to see. Because the Lord will bring to light what I am covering up, for all the world to see. God will do a spiritual surgery on you without anesthesia. He will expose your wounds, your motives, your intentions, and everything that you've been trying so hard to hide from everyone, to break you enough to let go of the pride that you are so desperately holding on to.

The Lord can expose that little child in you that you may be trying to cover up. You are trying to stuff that child down so that others won't see how immature and broken you are. Things that challenge you that you should have outgrown by now, that you are covering up so no one will know how you really feel. And that is exactly what God will do if you don't ask for help. He allows the enemy to expose all your shortcomings and fears and flaws if you don't humble yourself under His mighty hand. The enemy will come and create a situation that causes you to lose your cool, and let down your guard of all your secrets, and everyone will know the truth.

Rather than allowing the enemy to cause me to be exposed, pray before you open your mouth. Pray before you go into that meeting. Pray before you give an answer. Because the enemy is ready to strike and turn your pride into humiliation.

So, admit to God that you don't know everything, that you don't know all the answers. Admit when you are angry, or hurt, or worried. You don't have to pretend that you are perfect to God. Ask Him for His help and strength and guidance. When you feel that feeling of anger or hurt welling up inside you, turn to Him. Ask Him for help in managing those feelings so you don't humiliate yourself or hurt others.

Samson remained prideful. He knew the law and he knew that he was set apart by God. He knew he had taken the vow of a Nazarite. Yet he still allowed himself to fall asleep in the lap of Delilah. He ignored the rules and she cut his hair. The Lord had to break him to use Him. And God did use Samson for His glory, but it was too late for Samson. The pillars came down, and God could use him no more.

I'm a preacher, but I don't want to be only used on Sundays and Wednesdays. I want to be used by God everywhere and every day.

## CHAPTER TWELVE
*"No More Denial"*

Peter was one of Jesus' closest friends. But Peter had pride. He still cared about what people thought. And Jesus had to break him of that pride. And it broke Peter's heart. But after his pride was broken, God was able to use him. But he had to go through a painful process of exposure and humiliation before he got to that point. He lied three times and the rooster started crowing. And after that pain and humiliation Peter's heart was changed and God used him in mighty ways. He became the cornerstone of the church.

The Pharisees never admitted their brokenness and pride. So when we don't admit and turn from our pride, it doesn't matter how many times we sit in church. It doesn't matter how many Bibles we own. It doesn't matter how many tracts we hand out. If we don't break our pride, we will stand before judgment. It doesn't matter how religious we look on the outside. It doesn't matter if people see us giving out food boxes and helping the poor if we are only doing it to make a name for ourselves and looking for the praise of man. "It is a fearful thing to fall into the hands of the living God." (Hebrews 10:31)

"Therefore, it says, 'God opposes the proud but gives grace to the humble.' Submit

yourselves therefore to God..." (James 4:6-7) When we humble ourselves, He gives grace. He resists the proud. So our pride will be broken, one way or another. And when we die we will stand before God. We will have our pride broken then. Bragging about our good works won't get us anywhere. As the projector of our lives plays back and you see the things that you are being judged for, all the mistakes made and sins that you chose, you will realize that you knew better. And you will wish you had humbled yourself before Him.

So, to rebuke the spirit of pride, the first step is to acknowledge that you have a problem. No more denial.

What if I went to the doctor, and when they started doing their exam and taking my blood pressure and checking my pulse, they asked me to tell them what is wrong and what brought me in there that day. What if I said that I was absolutely fine and nothing was wrong? They may think that is odd. They check my blood pressure and tell me it is 175/100. And I say I'm fine. They tell me my sugar is over

400 and ask me if I'm feeling okay. And I say that there is nothing wrong with me. That's denial. I can't get well if I don't admit there is a problem. And it's the same with pride. We must admit that we have a problem.

Sometimes we don't want to talk about our past, or where we came from and what we went through. I don't have a problem talking about where I came from. Thank the Lord, I'm not there now. I'm not trying to hide it or stuff it down. I'm not trying to cover it up and pretend that it was different. I came from nothing. I don't let my pride tell me that's something I should be ashamed of. I'm not trying to impress anyone. I'm just trying to live my life honestly and humbly for the Lord.

Every human being struggles with pride. It's inevitable. Not all pride is evil. Have you ever washed your car, and you took pride in how good it looked, because you are paying a lot for the note on that vehicle and when you see that clean and shiny car you know it is worth it. And you feel a sense of accomplishment.

Or when you take pride in your work vehicle. So you keep it clean, and you wash the dirt off, even though you know you are going to have to go down that gravel road again. You want it to look good and you want to take care of it. That's not evil pride. That is just taking pride in what you do. In a job well done. It's being a good steward of what God has given you.

It's like fear. Fear is not always a bad thing. There is a right kind of fear. If you pull out in front of truck and almost get into an accident, you will be afraid. That is a healthy fear. If a bear comes running toward you and is standing on his hind legs in front of you and fear causes you to run to get away, that is a healthy fear.

But the spirit of fear is different. It will challenge you to question everything that God promises. It will keep us from stepping out on faith.

Fear is not evil; the spirit of fear has dire consequences and is destructive.

It is the same with pride. Pride is not in itself evil. But the spirit of pride can cause you to lose your soul. So, we need to take an honest look at ourselves. At our motives. We need to admit to ourselves what we are really feeling and thinking. We need to examine our attitudes and ask the Lord to reveal to us where pride is creeping in and causing problems. We need to ask God for help.

You may say, "I don't have that kind of pride in me." Yes, you do. You just proved it by denying it. If you think you don't have it, you do. Every one of us has an issue with pride. But not everyone admits it and is willing to do the work of humbling yourself to get rid of it. And it's never our place to judge others for their pride. We all have enough of our own to deal with. When we say we don't have a problem, that's when it will come sneaking up on us and before we know it, we are deep in it.

Pride can be subtle. Especially in marriages and families. "I'm not going to put up with that." "I'm going to prove you wrong." "I'm not going to talk to you." "I'm going to give you the silent treatment." "I know better than you." "I deserve better." All those things are pride.

# CHAPTER THIRTEEN
## *"Help Us, Lord!"*

Sometimes when dealing with people we must prove that we are right. Sometimes at work I might have a customer with an awful attitude. And instead of engaging with them I choose to let someone else deal with them. Because when dealing with people like that it's sometimes hard not to retaliate. Because sometimes walking away feels like defeat, or even less of a man. But that's pride that is telling me that. Now this doesn't mean that we have to roll over and take everything. We don't have to be a doormat.

But there is a way to do it that is not filled with pride. You don't have to join in the ugliness. You don't have to argue back. You don't have to match word for word. One time I was talking to someone at work and trying to explain something to them. And this person was very upset and was going on and on and wouldn't let me get a word in edgewise, allowing me to explain the situation. And the person accused me of not caring. And I told them if I didn't care, I wouldn't be there. But there was no use arguing with them because they were so worked up. The next day they wanted to deal with me again, and I kindly told them that they had gotten smart with me the day before. They denied it. and I politely and gently told them that they need to learn how to talk to people differently when they are upset.

I didn't raise my voice or match their ugliness. I had compassion because I figured they probably had never had anyone tell them it was inappropriate. I wasn't mad. And they responded that they weren't trying to hurt my feelings. And I let them know that my feelings weren't hurt and that I have a thick skin. So, we both apologized, and the conversation ended well. I think at times God will allow us to see our pride through the actions of other people.

I could have been nasty right back and said some ugly things when they accused me of not caring. My pride could have made me angry. "How dare they say that about me." And I could have made the situation much worse. But I don't like to burn bridges. I don't want to get a reputation of doing things like that because it wouldn't honor the Lord. So sometimes its ok to take a little bit of abuse and keep your composure. Remember your character and integrity and just calmly talk. Don't let pride cause you to raise your voice and get loud so you can defend yourself and prove that they are wrong, and you are right. Shouting and getting worked up doesn't help anything. You can calmly draw the line but handle it in a godly way. Our job is not to humiliate others, even if they aren't treating us right. Humiliating others will only cause you to kill your witness for the Lord.

And we should never brag about putting someone in their place or telling someone off. That's pride. Pride can look like arrogance. It can be easily seen as bragging. It makes everything all about you. Every choice you make is about you. All you think about is you. It's selfishness. And pride always takes the form of selfishness.

Pride takes the form of not listening to others. Not being willing to consider that you may be wrong and that there may be a better way. That someone might know more than you. When you are in the car and someone tells you to take a left, but you keep going straight and 10 miles down the road you must turn around and take that turn, but now you are late because you didn't listen.

On the other hand, if you are driving and you know that someone missed a turn, don't wait 10 miles for them to figure it out and then say arrogantly, "Oh, I knew you missed your turn." That's pride too, trying to make you look smarter than them. The devil is clever in how he can bring out our different variations of pride.

Sometimes pride comes out in ways that we really don't expect. Sarcasm can be pride. Sarcasm is meant to put someone down. It is always making fun of someone. I don't watch a lot of late-night television because they are full of sarcasm. Everything and everyone are a joke. And they are paid millions of dollars to make fun of people.

It's hard to talk to people who are sarcastic all the time. You don't know when they are serious. You always have to question the motive if they are making fun of you.

Pride can also come in the form of not being able to move on from mistakes in life. Being trapped in the guilt and shame of your past. It's pride because you are hung up on the thought that everyone is always thinking about the way you used to be. It's that intoxication of what people think about you. And how much they are thinking about you. This type of pride is completely self-centered. Choosing to live in that misery, as if you are the worst person in the world and you believe that everyone secretly judges you. If Jesus has forgiven you (which He has) and you are still stewing in the pity pot of your past, not forgiving yourself, that is pride.

Pride can come in the form of secrets and hiding and covering things up that make us look bad. You hide your family from others because you are embarrassed of them, and you don't want them to embarrass you or reveal things about you that they know. We take ourselves too seriously. It's okay for people to know the real you, past mistakes, weird families, and all. I don't mind sharing weird things and silly things and embarrassing things with people. I know that I am human and real and I don't have to try to act like someone I am not. That is one of the ways that we can practice humility. Just be ourselves, exactly the way God made us.

We must practice humility or pride will take over. When we show humility, and accept ourselves for who we are, it makes it easier to accept others for who they are, imperfections and all. Your family that comes over only to eat all your food and then leave. It happens every time. It's been happening for years. Pride wants you to make a big deal about it and call them out on it. But humility says let it go. You know what to expect from them and you accept them as they are.

Pride is always out to get you. It's a principality that wants to take you out. Dwelling on the past is a form of pride when the past causes you to feel intitled.

Putting others down is a form of pride.

Constantly complaining is a form of pride as it is a way to draw attention to yourself.

Low self-esteem is a form of pride.

Wanting to control everything is a form of selfish pride.

We all know people who show these types of pride. We have these tendencies ourselves.

We must break and rebuke that spirit of pride. We do that by humbling ourselves and making choices that intentionally hurt that pride. We humble ourselves under the mighty hand of God. It might be uncomfortable. It may not be fun. We may have to do things we don't want to do and say things we don't want to say. Acknowledge your problems. Pray against the spirit of pride. And the devil won't like it. It will be challenging. You will resist changing. But the more you lean into God and pray, the more sensitive to pride we will become. We will recognize when it is flaring up and be able to resist it more. The more pride is exposed, the less power it has in our lives and in our hearts. And as we grow in humility, we are less prideful with others. Our relationships improve. We have more peace in our lives.

So don't let pride creep in. Psalm 139:23-24. Help us, Lord.

## CHAPTER FOURTEEN
### *"A False Sense of Maturity"*

Studying about the spirit of pride is almost like being born again—all over again. It is like a new life. It is a revelation. God's Word points at all of us. And I am so thankful His word is not hidden, but that we can know how to be delivered and set free. We can know how to be made whole so that the enemy can't trick us and make us believe we don't need to change—that we are fine.

I don't want to be okay.

I want to be right.

I want to be true.

So, I thank the Lord that people are delivered in the name of Jesus. I thank Him for the Word of God that shows us that we can not only do the works that He did, but greater works. But I am convinced that we will never be able to step into that calling unless we pray like we should. And we can't pray like we should unless we pray with the right spirit, which is a humble place in the Lord. We must humble ourselves under the mighty hand of God.

It is by His grace and mercy that I am who I am. Had it not been for grace I would not have made it this far in life. If you don't learn anything else from me, make sure you find the place in your home where you can bow down and talk to Him. Love Him with all your heart and thank Him for His grace and mercy. There is a joy in knowing that truth. That every good and perfect gift is from above.

Prayer isn't a burden. It is a privilege and a gift. Prayer to God is not hard. When we know the Lord, we have already escaped hell. So, there is nothing to fear in prayer.

I'm so thankful for the revelation of God in the scriptures. God is so good. But one of the things that pride does is it makes sure that we have the light pointing on ourselves. Pride disguises and hides itself in our hearts, but it comes out sometimes ugly, but sometimes subtle ways. It wants to stay hidden so that I can't identify or recognize it in me. It is camouflaged. It blends in with its surroundings so that it is hard to see. It travels in stealth mode. It's like that fighter jet that can't be made out on the radar.

The spirit of pride is slick. It is deceitful and tricky. It can sneak up on you and before you know it pride is sitting right beside you. It's in your lap. It's all over you, whispering its lies into your heart. It is a horrible principality that can destroy our lives. That is why we must rebuke the spirit of pride. Scripture tells us that we can deceive ourselves. I don't want to go through life fooling myself. I don't want to be a legend in my own mind.

One of the attributes of pride is a false sense of maturity. A person thinks they are fully mature, when really, they have a lot of growing to do. We all have growing to do I have areas that I need to grow in, and sometimes I don't realize it until someone uncovers it and shows it to me. We must be willing to admit when we are coming up short. I don't want to think I handled something with maturity when really, I've behaved badly.

Sometimes pride will be disguised as false humility. That is why it is so important to ask God to search us. To search our hearts, to see if He can find anything there that shouldn't be. We need Him to shine the light of heaven on our souls to see if anything is hiding there or lurking where it can't be seen. Because the heart is deceitful and desperately wicked. And we can deceive ourselves. So, we need to ask God to reveal that which doesn't please Him. If I'm unwilling to pray this, then I know I have pride. And if I try to cover it up, He may not only reveal it, but He may expose it publicly. I would much rather have it revealed to me privately than be humiliated publicly, because the light will always shine on the darkness.

I don't mind being under the authority of another person. Submitting to the authority of others is often hard. Some people find it more difficult than others, not being able to work under other people. They would rather do things their way than have to listen to others.

Submission can be a challenge. But in our lives, we must come to the place where we learn to accept that sometimes we must submit to authority. If you can't work under someone, you will have a hard time keeping a job. We all know that person who goes from job to job to job because he never likes working under someone. And it's always the boss' fault in their eyes. You must come to the place where you realize that they hired you to do work, collect a check and go home. Not to run the place and tell them how it's supposed to be done in your eyes. You don't own the company. You're not the boss. You are supposed to submit to their authority and learn to take instruction and follow directions.

But the spirit of pride will keep you from being able to take instruction. Pride tells you that you are too good for that. That you already know everything, and you don't need to be told what to do. You don't need to keep learning, or growing, or changing. Pride does not allow for a teachable spirit.

Yes, you can and should read the Bible on your own. But the Bible also tells us that we should sit under the authority of sound preaching. Charles Smith says that he can't preach unless he can discern what the word of God is saying by the Holy Ghost. The pastor can't preach to you and teach you unless there is a burden on him, a demand on him, that comes from the anointing of God. God tells him what to say because of the condition of those he preaches to. When a person comes to sit under the preaching of God, the leader ought to feel something, to hear from the Holy Ghost. But if the leader is not submitted to the authority of the Lord, he will choose to stick with his notes, instead of saying what God wants him to say.

That's not to say that a pastor shouldn't be prepared and needs follow the Spirit's lead. But there should be a willingness to go in the direction that the Holy Ghost tells him to go and forget the notes if prompted by the Lord. Maybe the leader should forget the plan and the original thoughts and points he was going to make, because someone in the crowd needs to hear something different, according to the Holy Ghost. God says to forget that great idea you had and submit to Me and I will tell you what to say.

The pastor must submit.

## CHAPTER FIFTEEN
### *"Self-Will and Stubbornness"*

*"Obey them that have the rule over you, and submit yourselves: for they watch for your souls, as they that must give account, that they may do it with joy, and not with grief: for that is unprofitable for you."*

—HEBREWS 13:17

*"Likewise, ye younger, submit yourselves unto the elder. Yea, all of you be subject one to another, and be clothed with humility: for God resisteth the proud, and giveth grace to the humble."*

—1 PETER 5:5

*"And they continued stedfastly in the apostles' doctrine and fellowship, and in breaking of bread, and in prayers."*

—ACTS 2:42)

*"Not forsaking the assembling of ourselves together, as the manner of some is; but exhorting one another: and so much the more, as ye see the day approaching."*

—Hebrews 10:25

If you claim to be submissive, but you are not, that is false humility. We are to be accountable. Many people resist accountability. But there is value in accountability. I am my brother's keeper. And sometimes I need a brother to keep his eye on me. I want my friends to be able to check up on me and give me their honest opinions on how I am doing. To tell me when I'm going down the right path. We must humble ourselves and accept that we need people in our lives to help keep us in line. We need each other.

Sometimes I have to go into someone's house to do some work. And if the atmosphere seems not safe or seems like there is something to be wary of, I may take a friend for accountability. I want to be above even the appearance of evil.

Some people want to be independent, but they are uncommitted. There is nothing wrong with independence, but the spirit of pride will make you feel independent, but really you just won't commit to anything. You are unreliable and self-centered. You can never be on time. You don't do what you say you will. And you are full of excuses.

It's very hard to be around people like that. They don't make very good friends. People who are independent and uncommitted also feel like they don't need anyone to help them with anything. But if I am committed to something, and it is important to me, I want all the help I can get so the result will be good. But pride will make you want to do it on your own. It will make you want all the glory.

Pride makes you want all the accolades.

In a basketball game, trying to get all the glory for yourself doesn't end well. It works better if you depend on your team and work together. No one likes a ball hog, especially one who has an inflated view of how good they are. Don't go for all the credit and glory. If the team wins, you will all get the credit. Everyone wins.

We need each other. We do things together. We pray together. We worship together. It's not about just one of us. There is unity. Unity and community help face and overcome the obstacles that the devil throws on our path. You pray for me, and I pray for you. We depend on each other and challenge each other. And then, together, we watch God change things.

"Through desire a man, having separated himself, seeketh and intermeddleth with all wisdom." (Proverbs 18:1)

"He hath shewed strength with his arm; he hath scattered the proud in the imagination of their hearts. He hath put down the mighty from their seats, and exalted them of low degree." (Luke 1:51-52.)

Another attribute of pride is self-will and stubbornness. And it's amazing how many people I have heard boast about being stubborn. But God wants to change our stubbornness into steadfastness. Stubbornness can come from only wanting to do something or listen to someone of a certain status. Our pride tells us that we are too good to do anything or listen to anyone below that level.

Stubbornness makes it hard for us to cooperate with certain people, even if they want to help us. You stubbornly refuse to like a person's idea, simply because of who they are. You don't accept their help because you look down on them. But just because you don't appreciate someone else's values and insight on things, that doesn't make you right all the time. Pride tells us that we are always right.

People are stubborn about who cooks the macaroni and cheese for special events. Everyone thinks theirs is the best. There are so many ways to make mac and cheese today. So many cheeses to choose from. But if it's not yours, it's wrong. Now, when I was growing up, there was only hoop cheese. So, to me, that's the right way to make mac and cheese. But that doesn't mean that I am right. Or other versions aren't good.

We must humble ourselves. We must appreciate diversity. God made us different, with different tastes, talents, and interests. We need to appreciate our differences. I can appreciate what you do and what you have, even if I don't want it for myself.

Look at hair. People have different haircuts. Some I like better than others. Some I would never get for myself. But that doesn't mean that they are wrong because they don't get the same hair cut as I have. I can appreciate the diversity.

Another attribute of the spirit of pride is being critical. Thinking and talking negatively about other folks. And pride tells me that when I throw shade on others, it throws light on me. When I throw darkness on them, it throws the sunlight on me. And we find it so easy to evaluate someone instead of encouraging him.

I don't want to have to criticize people to make myself feel big. And when we hang around critical people, before we know it, we will start to love the gossip, and the information we hear from them, and we will become critical too. We will become nosy and ready to hear and talk about others.

Instead, we should mind our own business and pray for people instead of criticizing them behind their backs. When someone calls you on the phone to spread some craziness about another person, don't get sucked in. Refuse to listen. Instead pray for that person. Tell the person that called to pray for the person he is talking about. Stop the gossip in its tracks. If you do that, people will eventually stop trying to gossip with you.

## CHAPTER SIXTEEN
### *"We Are Called to Walk By Faith"*

Another attribute of pride is belittling someone. Pride makes us feel justified in putting someone in their place, so we can feel and look good. Ask God to search your heart to reveal if your motives are pure. We wouldn't want our motives to be blocking a blessing that God wants to shower over us.

This is especially true for people who lead. Leaders must be careful not to put other people down to build themselves up. When you are in a position of leadership or authority, you have to be careful. You must humble yourself, so you don't feel puffed up by knowing the secrets and the bad stuff about other people. You can't allow your position to cause you to feel superior. If you aren't careful your head will get bigger and bigger. Remember that you are only in that position because someone taught you and helped you, and God gave you grace. You didn't get there on your own. So, you have no right to feel superior.

When someone comes to you and doesn't know how to do something, humble yourself before you open your mouth. Remember that at one point in your life, you were right where they are. Someone had to show you and teach you. But pride will make you forget where you came from. It doesn't want you to remember your humble roots, whatever they may be. Poverty. Sin. Ignorance. Abuse. Addiction.

All of us have a story about our lives before we met the Lord. But pride doesn't want us to tell that story. Pride wants you to let people believe that your life has been great since the beginning. The devil is a liar, and we must rebuke that spirit so that our pride won't block what God intends for us.

The Lord wants to bless us more, but He won't because we limit ourselves in our pride. He can't get the blessings to us because we are participating in pride and being self-centered. We don't think we need Him. We think we can handle things on our own and we are doing just fine. We take credit for all the good in our lives and don't give God the glory, instead we lift ourselves up.

"He that is of a proud heart stirreth up strife: but he that putteth his trust in the Lord shall be made fat." (Proverbs 28:25)

A horrible attribute of pride is sowing discord, which means being divisive. When your attitudes and actions separate people and ruin relationships, families, connections, assassinate character, and destroy homes. When you like to stir the pot and get people all riled up at each other. What you are saying may not even be true, but you want to sow discord to make yourself look superior to others, having all the answers. When you take your words and undermine the confidence and trust in a person and cause others not to trust that person. When you spread lies. And people believe those lies and that gossip, without even giving that person a chance. And maybe that person was anointed by God, but because we believe the lies that are spread, we don't trust that person who God has called. And in doing so we hurt the ministry and even ourselves. We miss out on the blessings we would receive from the work of the anointed person who is being stifled because of discord.

The Lord hates all of this. The Lord wants us to be quiet unless we are going to say something positive and truthful. He does not want us to sow discord or spread division. We are supposed to be known by our love and unity, not our gossip and slander. Pride wants us to throw rocks and hide our hands. Pride wants us to say one little thing that will lead others to believe something about someone, and before you know it that one little thing has snowballed and wrecked relationships and robbed people of trust.

So, if you hear something, don't just automatically repeat it. I try not to believe things until I see it. If God doesn't reveal it to you, then don't worry about it.

"Whoso privily slandereth his neighbour, him will I cut off: him that hath an high look and a proud heart will not I suffer." (Psalm 101:5)

Elijah was a man of God. He was a mighty prophet of God. He had just called fire down from heaven. But he ran from what Jezebel said. He ran from her voice, her mouth, the message that was sent by her. He didn't even hear it from her voice firsthand. But he found out what she said she was going to do to him, and he ran. He knew that the words that poured from that mouth were like poison. Deadly poison. She was a slanderer, spreading evil.

Always remember the old saying, "if you can't say something nice, don't say anything at all."

"Their throat is an open sepulchre; with their tongues they have used deceit; the poison of asps is under their lips: Whose mouth is full of cursing and bitterness:" (Romans 3:13-14)

Another attribute of pride is disrespect. Having little respect for others. If you have a hard time encouraging or honoring someone else, you have a problem. If you can't celebrate other people, that is a pride issue. Be glad for someone when the Lord blesses them with a new job, or a new car, or a raise, even a new ministry. If you can celebrate someone else, without resentment or jealousy or pride, then maybe God will bless you in the same way. If people have what you can't afford, don't disrespect them, or tear them down in public, or even just in your heart, because you think you deserve what they have. The blessings of others should not bother you. You should be content with what you have.

But pride causes us to compare what we have to what others have. But we must trust God to give us what He sees fit to give. Sometimes by not giving us what we want, He is blessing us. Because some of those blessings that we see others receive would be a curse for us. God's ways are higher than our ways, and He can see the big picture that we cannot. Just because someone gives you a free Lamborghini does not mean it is blessing. What about when you have to spend $2000 on the oil change, or something breaks down and the part costs $5000. It could quickly turn into a curse.

A world of materialism will only bring you to a place of destruction. But we are called to walk by faith. And we know that God reigns on the just as well as the unjust, but the just shall live by faith. I want whatever the Lord decides is for me. Not what everyone else has.

"Now Korah, the son of Izhar, the son of Chetah, the son of Levi, and Dathan and Abiram, the sons of Eliab, and On, the son of Peleth, sons of Reuben, took men: And they rose up before Moses, with certain of the children of Israel, two hundred and fifty princes of the assembly, famous in the congregation, men of renown: And they gathered themselves together against Moses and against Aaron, and said unto them, Ye take too much upon you, seeing all the congregation are holy, every one of them, and the Lord is among them: wherefore then lift ye up yourselves above the congregation of the Lord?" (Numbers 16:1-3)

When you have a hard time encouraging and honoring others, because you want your turn, that is pride. It's not your time. Wait on the Lord. Let God validate you. I learned this lesson a long time ago. When I felt God's calling on my life, I had big dreams. I thought I would be a worldwide evangelist, traveling around. But a wise man asked me one simple question. "What about your children and your family?" And I thought about it and realized that I couldn't leave them to travel around. And that I was called to be a pastor to my family first and then the church. I had to wait on God and not just jump ahead and make assumptions of how He was going to use me.

## CHAPTER SEVENTEEN
*"Choose to Rebuke Pride and Follow God"*

When you get saved and filled with the Holy Ghost, you get excited! You are ready to storm hell with a water pistol, feeling you can do anything for God. And we can make assumptions about what God wants that are way off. And when we act on those assumptions, instead of waiting on the Lord, the so-called blessings can be a curse. So, we must listen and humble ourselves to do what God is asking us to do. Sometimes He is calling you to your family. It`s wise to be the leader of your home first before you can go out and reach others. Many get this out of order, and homes and families are lost because a person's priorities are messed up. One person thought they heard from God, and in their pride and zeal, they left their families to do what they thought was God's work. Due to a lack of balance and prioritization, failure is inevitable.

Another attribute of the spirit of pride is conflict.

When we find ourselves in personality conflict, not getting along with certain people, we must be willing to look at ourselves and see if it is caused by pride. It is okay to disagree with someone. And conflict can arise sometimes. There are valid issues that need to be addressed sometimes. But if you find yourself always at odds with people, and you always have a hard time getting along with people, then maybe the problem is you. If everyone is saying the same thing, and only you disagree, maybe you should look at yourself and ask God to search your heart for pride. Pride will never allow you to apologize to your spouse when you are wrong. You might even get a "lump in your throat".

There might be something in you, part of your personality, thoughts, or attitude, that needs to be adjusted. We must be willing to bring it to the Lord and ask Him to show us a true view of ourselves. Ask God to show you if you are causing people to walk on eggshells around you. Are you making people feel uncomfortable? Is there an ugliness in you that is apparent to others, but not to you? Have you been blaming others and pointing out their flaws, but really you are the problem?

"Only by pride cometh contention: but with the well advised is wisdom." Proverbs 13:10.

"Now therefore there is utterly a fault among you, because ye go to law one with another. Why do ye not rather take wrong? why do ye not rather suffer yourselves to be defrauded?" (1Corinthians 6:7)

Another attribute of pride is anger. Do you need anger management? Does every little thing make you angry? Do you regularly have to count to ten before you open your mouth? Do you feel that heat rising around the collar all the time? Do you want to "bite someone's head off"? Do you always have to be right?

Anger was given by God, and sometimes is justified. But we must manage it. Jesus got angry. When He went into the temple and the money changers were cheating people, he chased them out with a whip. He was angry, but He managed his anger. Anger is one of God's attributes. But He doesn't want us always gritting our teeth or biting our tongue because we are so mad at every little thing. He doesn't want us turning red with tears running down our face because we can't handle or manage our feelings of anger.

We need to pray about it. And just because we pray doesn't mean that people won't make us angry. We must pray and ask God to help us to respond differently. We all need this help. The devil will send someone along to pull your chain and to make you react in ways you know aren't godly. But when you have the Spirit of the living God in you, He will show up in you and give you the strength to respond in a way that pleases Him. You can respond with grace and mercy and love and peace. You don't have to stay angry. Even if the person you are angry with doesn't change, you can choose peace. Being easily angered and easily offended is not of the Lord. Easily crossed and ready to disagree is not of the Lord. Some people just have to get the last word in, no matter what you do or say. They must show you that they are right. If you say blue, they will say red. They want to live in conflict so that they can prove that you are not as smart as you think you are.

In this life we will encounter people with issues. They have personality problems or disorders. They may be narcissists. They may have bipolar disorder. Some of these people are very smart and very well educated. They are not stupid or dumb. They have emotional setbacks. They need deliverance and understanding. So, when you encounter them, what are you going to do? You can't run from them or avoid them if you live with them or work with them. You must be able to take it without responding in anger. And God will show you how to be like Jesus if you allow Him to.

"A scorner loveth not one that reproveth him: neither will he go unto the wise." (Proverb 15:12)

One of the attributes of pride is the inability to accept correction. Prideful people often love correcting other people, but the flip side of the coin is that they cannot successfully receive correction or suggestions of things that need to be changed. They can't handle constructive criticism. Some people take correction as an attack or a questioning of their character. They take it as if they are being degraded or rebuked. Correction is not necessarily a rebuke or an attack. Sometimes correction will save your life.

If someone tells you to stop walking in a certain direction, and you assume that they are telling you that because they think you are stupid, or that they are trying to control you, you may be endangering yourself by not listening to them. Because there may be an alligator in the path that you are walking down that the other person can see, but you can't. Their correction is only to help protect you.

They even tell you that there is a huge snake over there. And you tell them that you are going to walk wherever you want to walk and that you know all about gators. As if that will keep you safe. The gator doesn't care who you are or what you know. He's going to eat you. Don't let pride keep you from accepting corrections.

"He that covereth his sins shall not prosper: but whoso confesseth and forsaketh them shall have mercy." (Proverbs 28:13)

"Confess your faults one to another, and pray one for another, that ye may be healed. The effectual fervent prayer of a righteous man availeth much." (James 5:16)

Everybody struggles with pride. Some people can't admit They are wrong. They can't say they are sorry. They avoid apologizing at all costs. They make excuses.

When the COVID pandemic came, I wasn't afraid of dying. But it did make me sit back and think. If I were to go, I wanted to make sure I did it in the right way. If I offended anybody, I asked them to forgive me. I wanted to repent and make sure my life and my heart was right with the Lord. And we never know when that day will be when God calls us home. So repent. Change your mind. The devil wants to kill you and destroy your life. Choose to rebuke pride and follow God.

## CHAPTER EIGHTEEN
*"As Long As It Is Pleasing to the Lord"*

On my way to church, I pass a corn field. The crop of corn seems to go as far as the eyes can see. But the corn doesn't seem to be doing too well. Corn is ready to harvest when it dries. But if there isn't rain and the corn doesn't get nourished, it may dry too soon. The corn in this field looks like it is not filling out, or it's going dry before it matures. The crop may be lost.

How many of us are like that. Thinking we are mature, but really, we are dried up before we reach maturity because we aren't watered by the spirit of the Lord on a daily basis. We need prayer. We need to hide the word in our hearts. With today's technology, it has never been easier to feast on the word. Even if you are traveling, you can listen to an audio version. It is easy to feed yourself the things of God. But sometimes we get sidetracked because we have too much. Most of us have more "things" than we've ever had. We are busier than we've ever been. But we can't substitute material things for the nourishment that we need from God. Because God wants to bless us. He wants to talk to us, and He wants us to talk to Him. Pride keeps us from that.

One of the attributes of pride is when people struggle to admit when they are wrong or they don't know something, for fear of looking bad. They can't admit that they don't know. In humility we can admit that we don't know everything and be grateful for what we do know. Life should not be hinged on what someone else thinks about what I know or don't know. But pride keeps us intoxicated on the thoughts and opinions of others. We are drunk on what someone else thinks about us. We live for everyone else.

But I don't want to live for people. I want to live for the Lord. When you try to constantly figure out what people are thinking about you, you get in the habit of doing what you think they would want, and you end up living a fake life. A life that is more concerned with what you perceive that people want than what the Lord wants for you. And it's impossible to base your life on people's opinions because everyone is different. You will drive yourself crazy trying to please everyone if you must act differently around different people and personalities. And before you know it you have created 20 different versions of yourself.

But when we live for the Lord, there is only one version. The true me. It's so much easier that way. Instead of worrying about the clothes that I wear, only wearing what people like, I wear what I want to wear. My choices are not based on others. I get to choose what I like, as long as it is pleasing to the Lord. Humility will allow us to be comfortable in our own skin.

Pride wants us to be viewed a certain way by people and robs us of our true selves. It robs us of knowing who God created us to be. And the ironic thing is, when we try to please people so that they will see us in a certain way, it doesn't leave us satisfied. Because only the love of God can fulfill us. Instead of always trying to "get" from others, we should get our affirmation from God. And then humility allows us to esteem others higher than ourselves and treat them with the love of God. Because we are secure in ourselves because we see ourselves as God sees us. And the more we live like this, and practice this, the more the Lord will bless us and teach us.

The Lord teaches us how to humble ourselves and lift others up, so that He can exalt and lift us up. We need to practice building people up, instead of putting them down. You take the low seat. You become willing to be vulnerable. Preachers who are willing to be real and tell their life story–the good, the bad, and the ugly–are the ones who have the potential to reach the world. If you can't show your scars because of pride, and you refuse to reveal that you are a human who is imperfect, and who has made some mistakes, then that's a problem. That's pride.

The Holy Ghost will always tell you where the enemy is, but He won't necessarily save you from everything. We are human. We make mistakes. And the Lord lets us live life and deal with the consequences. One day, while working, I tripped and fell into a ladder. I stumbled. The Lord didn't warn me ahead of time to avoid walking that way. He lets us stumble. We are human. We fall. We make mistakes. We put our foot in our mouth. We don't have to pretend that we are perfect. This is true in the little things, and in the bigger more serious things that we have overcome through the grace and strength of God. So don't be afraid of people knowing your scars and your past.

It's okay to revisit your scars. They are healed. And they are a reminder of how good God is and what He has brought you through. But some people don't want to look at their scars. They don't want them to be exposed. They want to deny that they are even there. They want to cover them up.

In your life you have been hurt. Maybe people have hurt you or treated you badly. You don't have to pretend that you were never wounded. Because sometimes your revelation of where you've been and what you overcame will be the victory for another person. And if you don't allow others to see your scars, you are robbing them of the truth that can make them free and offer them healing. You can't help them if you want to look perfect on the outside. When we have a story, we are supposed to share it, so we can bring people to the Lord. You won't bring anyone to the Lord if they can't relate to how good God is because you are pretending to be perfect.

You need a story. You need a testimony. He did bring you out of sin and pain. What did God stop you from doing? What did He save you from? Don't let pride keep you from telling your story of God's grace and power in your life.

## CHAPTER NINETEEN
### *"We Don't Have to Promote Ourselves"*

> *"Whoso loveth instruction loveth knowledge: but he that hateth reproof is brutish."*
>
> —PROVERBS 12:1

Pride will make you unteachable. You won't pursue or accept correction because correction will cause anger in you. You will not be able to sit under leadership with the right attitude. Your ego will cause you to believe that you know more than the teacher.

Pride will make me think I can go anywhere and do anything. That I can march right into your house and go into your refrigerator and grab a cold drink and then sit down, lean back, and put my feet on the kitchen table. Even though it is your house. Pride causes entitlement. And when you question me or dare to ask me to take my feet off your table and not go through your fridge without permission, pride causes me to get angry. How dare you!

In pride we often think rules don't apply to us. The door says exit only, but we ignore that and go in anyway. The sign says one way, but we go the wrong way anyway and end up causing problems. We are inconsiderate. People get mad at us. But pride tells us that is their problem, not ours.

Pride causes us to be slow to repent. We are slow to ask for forgiveness. If you can't ask for forgiveness, you will always carry the wounds of others. You must learn to apologize when you are wrong. It's hard to admit when we are wrong. I often have to say it out loud to myself. "Sometimes I am wrong." You should try it sometime.

Sometimes we are wrong. It doesn't always mean that we did something maliciously. Sometimes we just assume we are right about something until something, or someone shows us that it's not true. We are human. We make assumptions. We didn't see clearly. We didn't have all the information. We were wrong. But pride will cause you not to admit it. We must practice admitting when we are wrong.

We must be careful about only listening to people of a certain status. I've heard people say that they won't listen to a pastor who doesn't have a master's degree. And when I hear that, I think about Jesus. He was 12 years old, teaching in the temple, asking questions, astounding the doctors, and being led by the spirit of God. And the people marveled at His wisdom. Because the Holy Ghost always supersedes what we learn from books. Even if you have had the good fortune to have a great education, it means nothing if you don't have the wisdom to apply it. All the education in the world does no good if we don't have common sense. All the honors, awards, banners and prestige of an education mean nothing if you can't learn to work hard and do the simple things in life.

Sometimes we classify people by their level of prestige. But prestige does not equate wisdom. We put them on a pedestal and compare ourselves to them. We want to be around them because their lives seem more glamorous and exciting than ours do. They have nice things and drive fancy cars and have great careers. And we don't want to hang around people who are more simple, less educated, less wealthy. We judge others. That's pride. And it is not our job to judge. God loves everyone equally. Everyone has value. Everyone has something to offer. We can't look down on people and refuse to let them in our lives because of our judgment of their status. Their prestige has nothing to do with their soul.

Pride will make us fall into a trap. But humility will give us eyes to see all people as souls that belong to the Lord.

Whether they are rich or poor. Black or white. Old or young. Educated or not. We can't pick and choose which people are "worthy" of our friendship based on these things. We can't exclude people based on materialistic and worldly ideals. God gives us the wisdom to be able to equally love and relate to every man. He wants us to always be ready with an answer of how God loves and saved us. We aren't too good for anyone. We aren't above anyone.

We are the light of the world. We can't pass someone by because of how he looks or acts and leave him to lose his soul. We must care about the souls of everyone. Someone cared for my soul, and I'm so thankful for that. So, leave room in your life to care about other people.

A good way to care about others, regardless of who they are, is to practice doing random acts of kindness. Doing this helps release us of our pride and ego. It helps us be less self-centered and more willing to give.

Pride only wants a one-way ticket. We only want to receive. We only do something so that someone will do something for us. There is always a selfish motive. What can I get out of it. If we aren't getting something from it, we will never reach out to anyone, and always looking for reciprocation.

I often remind church members to be good tippers at restaurants, and to see the workers as souls. Not just people who are serving you. Because I learned that if you leave a good tip regularly, you will have a good reputation with the workers. And they will want to serve you. And when they see you as a good person, maybe they will get to know you and you can share the love of Jesus with them. They will listen to you, because they know that you have a good heart and you have blessed them before. So, they have a certain amount of trust in you. And they may be willing to listen to what you have to say. But if you leave bad tips regularly, then call yourself a Christian, that is not a great testimony. We must humble ourselves and see people as souls, desperate for God. Not just people that we can use and exploit. Not see them as people who owe us anything.

Pride makes us reveal things about ourselves that wisdom would have us keep quiet about. We want people to know all the things we know. We want to impress them. We brag about our knowledge, experience, and abilities. But the Bible tells us that we don't have to promote ourselves. That our gifts will do that for us.

I learned this the hard way when I was younger. I was immature and eager to impress. I got a job and proved everything I knew. And I tried to help everyone else with their jobs, and they found out how much I could do. And after a while I was doing the job of three men but getting one man's salary. I should have kept my mouth shut. But instead, I wanted to feel important and needed. But that led to me being used and manipulated. And it was my fault. I did it to myself. They would never have expected me to do all that work if I hadn't bragged about how well I multitasked and knew so much.

So, what did I really accomplish in all that pride? I ended up quitting that job. Because I realized that I was being taken advantage of and not being paid enough. When I tried to promote myself and prove to them my worth, instead of just doing the job I was asked to do, I got manipulated and used. Wisdom and humility taught me that I don't have to self-promote. It might not be the right time to expose all that I know and have done. Wisdom tells me to keep quiet about my gifts and talents. God will exalt me.

I don't have to step up to every volunteer opportunity that there is. Sometimes when we get so busy doing good things, we miss out on the GREAT thing that God has for us.

## CHAPTER TWENTY
*"We Don't Need to Join Every Argument"*

*"A fool hath no delight in understanding, but that his heart may discover itself."*

—PROVERBS 18:2

Pride makes you think that you always should speak your mind. Sometimes you need to keep it to yourself. But in pride we feel we have the right to say every little thing we think. That our opinion always needs to be heard. That we have the solution to every problem, and they need to hear it. Sometimes we are like this because we feel like we have been shoved aside in life, so we must reveal how smart we are.

When I come across someone like this, I try not to feel the urge to impress them with how much I know. I just let them talk. I might know the right answer, but I don't have to prove that to someone. God didn't create me to always have to be right. And He gives me wisdom and tells me when to open my mouth and when to shut it. If I know a person is going to disagree with me, sometimes the wise decision is to not get involved in the conversation or offer a rebuttal. So, I keep it to myself.

It's like I said about tipping the server in a restaurant. People are watching. You are representing Christ. We attract people more with humility than by being a know-it-all. We don't need to join every argument, especially when we know it's not going to change anything. They aren't going to be swayed by your opinion. They just like to hear themselves talk. I get that. I'm a preacher. I'm used to talking. But in humility I can let someone else have the floor. We don't have to feel like we are the only ones to have the answer.

"Behold, this was the iniquity of thy sister Sodom, pride, fulness of bread, and abundance of idleness was in her and in her daughters, neither did she strengthen the hand of the poor and needy."(Ezekiel 16:49)

"They are enclosed in their own fat: with their mouth they speak proudly." (Psalm 17:10)

Pride is revealed in us when we treat people poorly. When the gas station cashier doesn't greet you properly or use common manners and is just on their phone or talking to their coworker. When you ask them a question and they look at you like you are an inconvenience, and they have an attitude when they answer. "Pump five isn't taking my card." And they answer back that it must have been something you did. "Well, can you help me?" Pride will have them roll their eyes as if they are too good to help you. Humility would sound like this: "Yes, sir, I will do whatever I can to help. I will cancel your transaction at the pump and run your card for you myself."

In pride we can treat people coldly and harshly. We can be hard and rigid. But when we claim the name of Jesus, we don't want to kill our witness. Pride will ruin our witness for the Lord. They will think less of God because of the way we act when we are supposed to be like Him. It doesn't matter if you walk around carrying a Bible to show you are a Christian. What matters is how you treat people. If you treat people poorly, word will get around and your witness will be useless because people won't want anything that you have. They don't want to be like you. And they will let everyone know the type of person you are. They will ruin your reputation as you have killed your witness.

As a preacher, I think people watch me to see if I practice what I preach. They watch to see if I will make a mistake, or fall, or say something wrong. Some people feel like they have a license to be a Holy Ghost checker. They don't really want Jesus, but they feel like it's their job to make sure the pastor doesn't step out of line. And they judge everything I say or do to see if I slip up so they can prove that I'm a hypocrite. When I started Agape Worship Center, I was new to leadership. I needed guidance from an experienced leader, but I didn`t realize that for a few years. I was somewhat rigid and very direct with a stern facial expression. At times, I might have even handled ministry issues wrong. That was an example of sincere ignorance rather than pride. I saw other leaders and their actions, and I started to think wrong. I thought that as a pastor, I should have a certain car, or live a certain way, and associate with certain people. That thought process led to a prideful life unaware. It was a subtle and sneaky spirit that crept in and tried to destroy me, but the Lord will always show Himself faithful if you ask Him to "show you to you". The Devil will try to get you to idolize yourself and prove things to others. Then that same demon will trick you with ideas of becoming great using deception about your future. I will associate it with the spirit of Python.

The intent is to have you indulge in self-worship of your own abilities and ideas. This prideful spirit will wrap itself around you and squeeze out your joy, your worship, your praise, as well as your prayer-life and you will think that you are doing God`s service.

If you humble yourself, you don't have to prove anything. Just live for the Lord. When they see you, they will see the fruit of the spirit coming forth from you. So let them say what they want. Let them watch God work in your life while you humble yourself.

"And it came to pass, as he went to Jerusalem, that he passed through the midst of Samaria and Galilee. And as he entered into a certain village, there met him ten men that were lepers, which stood afar off: And they lifted up their voices, and said, Jesus, Master, have mercy on us. And when he saw them, he said unto them, Go shew yourselves unto the priests. And it came to pass, that, as they went, they were cleansed. And one of them, when he saw that he was healed, turned back, and with a loud voice glorified God, And fell down on his face at his feet, giving him thanks: and he was a Samaritan. And Jesus answering said, Were there not ten cleansed? but where are the nine? There are not found that returned to give glory to God, save this stranger. And he said unto him, Arise, go thy way: thy faith hath made thee whole." (Luke 17:11-19)

"Speaking to yourselves in psalms and hymns and spiritual songs, singing and making melody in your heart to the Lord; Giving thanks always for all things unto God and the Father in the name of our Lord Jesus Christ;" (Ephesians 5:19-20)

Another attribute of pride is being ungrateful. Sometimes we allow this spirit to be embedded in our children. We give them everything they want. We spoil them so much that they think they are entitled to everything, and they aren't grateful. In some cases, they don't appreciate what you do for them.

This is also true in adults. Our expectations are too high. We feel entitled. We expect people to bend over backwards to give us what we want or need.

Another attribute of pride is perfectionism. A perfectionist is never satisfied. A perfectionist has to have everything a certain way. Their way. They expect perfection from themselves and from others. But deep-down perfectionism masks how inferior they feel. So, they overcompensate to make everything seem perfect.

Humility lets us recognize our limited abilities. It lets us try something new and make mistakes and learn along the way. It knows that sometimes failure is a part of life and can teach us and improve our lives if we learn the lesson. But perfectionists can't admit weakness and will have a hard time accepting the weaknesses of others. They will have trouble making friends. They will never allow themselves to be in friendships with people that they can glean from and advise them. When you turn your back on them, they will tear you down. They will look for reasons to not accept you. They are looking for flaws.

When someone is focused on looking for flaws, then flaws will be all they see. If you buy a used car, even for a great price, and you look it over to look for flaws, flaws will be all you see. And you won't buy the car, even though it's a great deal, but it's not perfect.

It's the same with churches. There is no perfect church. There is no perfect preacher. But people use that as an excuse not to go to church. If you are constantly looking for flaws, and you look hard enough, you will find them every time. Because no one is perfect.

When we go to buy something from a store, we check it first to make sure there isn't anything wrong with it. Just because something is flawed, it doesn't mean it needs to be thrown away. And just because people are flawed doesn't mean that they aren't lovable. It doesn't mean they are all bad. We must accept that the world that we are living in isn't perfect. It is flawed. Jesus understands that and loves us. And flawed people that He loves should also understand that.

Pride causes us to look for flaws. Instead see people as Jesus sees them—souls to be loved. And we must pray to God to help us with this attribute of perfectionism. Perfectionism can present itself in many forms. We may be obsessed with looking perfect. You may be obsessed with making a perfect cake, and when there is one little flaw, you throw the whole thing away.

We weren't meant to be perfect. It's simply not possible.

Pride can make us feel entitled or deserving. It causes us to get puffed up. We present ourselves in a certain way. I've seen people practice a walk, or an accent so they can present themselves a certain way, and this makes them feel important or entitled. They are entitled to choose the restaurant. They are entitled to be under the umbrella while everyone else gets rained on. They are entitled to park in the spot right in front of the door. Because that's how they feel. They simply deserve certain luxuries in life.

Pride will keep you self-focused. You come first, before anyone else. Your needs and wants are what is most important to you. You lack compassion for others. To get out of this type of pride, we need to practice doing things for other people. And we need to allow other people in our lives to do things for other people, without becoming jealous. Don't be jealous you're your friends do something for someone else instead of you.

Deceit is a form of pride. Deceit is more than just telling a bold-faced lie. We can work deceit. It is when we deliberately intend to make people believe something that isn't true. When someone asks you to stop by the store and get them something and you forgot. And when they asked if you got it, you find a way to spin the truth without lying, so that you look better. You make them think something besides the truth.

We also can put words in other people's mouths. They can say something, and we can twist their words so they mean something completely different. To put their words in a different light for others to see.

We can tell half-truths. Someone calls your cell phone at 3:00 and you see it ringing, but you don't want to answer it. And later when you talk to that person, and they ask why you didn't answer, you tell them your phone was in the car.

These little deceits may look small. But God does not like deceit. So just answer truthfully. "I saw your call but I didn't pick it up because I was driving". "Or, I saw your call, but it wasn't a good time for me". "I saw your message, but I haven't had time to call you back". Don't be deceitful.

God help us if we are comfortable practicing deceit. Those little white lies. Practicing deceit will lead to rationalization. We begin to believe that it is okay. And we do it more and more. Instead of just admitting that we didn't answer the phone because it was not a good time. Rather than making something up, I can just tell the truth, that I was unavailable, but I'm available now. How can I help you?

When you practice deceit, you practice manipulation by making people think what you want them to think. You twist the truth a little bit.

When you have something white, and you mix another color in with it, it changes the color. And the more you mix it with another color, and add to it, the less white it is. And before you know it there is no trace of white and you can't even recognize what it originally looked like.

Pride does this to us. We need to rebuke the spirit of pride and choose to be humble, so the Lord can exalt us in due season. He wants to bless us. And don't confuse blessings with material things. Blessings are so much more. Spending time with the Lord is a blessing. Hearing from heaven is a blessing. Walking in His will is a blessing. Being delivered from the spirit of pride is a blessing.

# Endnotes

[1] John 3:30, KJV
[2] Matthew 13:55, KJV
[3] Matthew 8:20, KJV
[4] Isaiah 53:2, KJV
[5] Luke 22:27, KJV
[6] John 5:30, KJV

www.ingramcontent.com/pod-product-compliance
Lightning Source LLC
Chambersburg PA
CBHW071701040426
42446CB00011B/1860